– *Table of Contents* –

THE URGENCY OF
BIBLICAL MANHOOD

~~~~~

Max Sherman was an unknown energy-efficiency scientist, until he ran some tests on an iconic product. As a specialist in examining the effectiveness of sealants within heating and air conditioning systems, he made a startling discovery that he reported in a small circulation publication, *Home Energy Magazine*. His finding, however, was picked up by *USA Today*, then *Wall Street Journal* and then a frenzy of media outlets.

His discovery was that most duct sealants were relatively effective with one notable exception: duct tape. Sherman reported that duct tape "failed reliably and often quite catastrophically" when applied to duct systems.

He blogged about the kinds of question he started getting regularly along with his routine answers. Question #1: "How did duct tape get its name?" Sherman: "I don't know." Question #2: "What can you use it for?" Sherman: "Anything but ducts." Question #3: "Do you use duct tape?" Sherman: "All the time, just not on ducts." [1]

What made Sherman's story so newsworthy is the incessant joking that surrounds duct tape and how it's thought to be the stuff that holds the whole world together. "Popular culture abounds with uses for duct tape: duct tape calendars, books like *101 Uses for Duct Tape*, and more,"[2] stated Max's report, "But lab experiments have finally proved that duct tape, as it is generally used, should not be used to seal ducts." And so we find that duct tape is good for many applications but cannot fulfill its original purpose — what it was created for and what it was named after. The irony of the naming and usage of duct tape is the same irony that is played out in men's lives across the nation week after week. There's a lot men can do, but they are struggling to do what they were created for.

[1] How duct tape sealed my place in history http://www.aps.org/publications/apsnews/199812/sherman.cfm

[2] Can Duct Tape Take the Heat? http://homeenergy.org/archive/hem.dis.anl.gov/eehem/98/980710.html

We need *men*

—

If ever there was a time we needed men to know their purpose and to be men again, it's now.

Our world is filled with great uncertainty and instability and leaders are hard to find. We need men who aren't preoccupied with their amusements or appearance, but instead are willing and able to take on manly challenges.

But it's not enough for men to take up manly activities here and there. Men abound who can do manly stuff (like shave with a straight razor, build fires without matches, and deep fry turkeys) while still being disengaged where their leadership is needed most. Every day, men hide behind computer screens or pleasure pursuits instead of engaging.

We need men with consistent character: integrity, courage, perseverance, and a willingness to sacrifice and lead for the greater good.

We need men *of God*

—

We've written this book, however, with a major distinction from other manhood resources. We're convinced that what we need most are men of God.

We need men who won't just stand up, but will stand on something solid and timeless.

In a relativistic world, men need to understand who God designed them to be, how they are prone to sin in their manhood because of the fall and how Jesus came to redeem them as men.

We need men of God *who are doers of the Word*

—

We've also written this because we've seen too many men with great gaps between their beliefs and behaviors on biblical manhood. We need men of God who are active and consistent in living out their faith.

"Be doers of the word," says James, "and not hearers only, deceiving yourselves" (Jas 1:22). It doesn't matter what you believe about God or biblical manhood if it doesn't make a meaningful difference in the way you live — in the classroom, on the job, as a husband, or as a father.

This guidebook is all about practical theology — the doing of the word.

We provide recommended reading in the resource section for anyone who wants to learn more about biblical manhood, but what you'll mostly see in these pages are practical ways to live it out every day of your life, to push past the barriers that often separate belief from behavior.

We realize this kind of practical application of biblical manhood can be seen as subjective. We're not going to say that acting on all the specifics of this guidebook is the only effective way to demonstrate biblical manhood. We are convinced, however, that beliefs have to result in action. The last thing the world needs is men with great insights on biblical manhood sitting on the sidelines [or worse, acting in ways that contradict what they believe].

We need men of God who are doers of the Word *for the sake of the gospel*

—

Ultimately, however, we wrote this book because we believe that biblical manhood has to lead to urgency for the sake of the gospel.

We need men who will shoulder the weight of manhood as God designed it, who will live it out day to day but will incline their manhood toward the gospel.

It is the gospel that saves men — as Jesus replaces their sin and rebellion with his righteousness — and it's what makes it possible for men to be redeemed in their masculinity and to serve God with all of their manhood. And it's for the sake of the gospel that redeemed men have a new commission for their leadership — to proclaim the good news and make disciples.

Instead of compartmentalizing the gospel, redeemed men are to see it intersecting with their life at work, in their marriage and with their kids. And pastors who understand this intersection as well shouldn't see cultivating redeemed men as a distraction from the Gospel but see it as a primary front for advancing the good news.

The gospel needs of our world today provide unlimited opportunities for both men and women to serve. But so many of the needs — in rapidly growing urban centers, among unreached people groups and so on — require a kind of courage, toughness, and self sacrifice, that God gifted men to bring.

And so we pray this book will admonish, encourage and instruct you to be a man of God who is a doer of the Word for the sake of the gospel.

RANDY STINSON & DAN DUMAS

LESSONS IN
BIBLICAL MANHOOD

~~~~

Discerning manhood from men of the Bible

—

"All Scripture is breathed out by God and profitable for teaching, for reproof, for correction, and for training in righteousness, that the man of God may be competent, equipped for every good work" (2 Timothy 3:16-17).

Throughout the pages of the Bible, men of God can find the instruction they need to be competent and equipped for every good work. Numerous lessons for biblical manhood surround the key men of the Bible. As we consider their lives within the full counsel of Scripture, we find examples for how men should live, lead, and respond to challenges and temptations and conversely how men shouldn't live, lead, and respond to challenges and temptations.

Much has been written about the men of the Old and New Testaments: Abraham, Joseph, Moses, Samson, Elijah, Jeremiah, Daniel, John the Baptist, Peter, Timothy, and others. In this guide, we're going to focus on five significant men of the Bible — Adam, Job, David, Solomon, and Paul. Because of the ways they lived out their manhood, these men profoundly shaped both history and eternity.

Each of these men also fell short. Adam's fall made fallen men out of all of us. David and Solomon violated horribly some of the principles and proverbs for which they are most known. In their failure, however, these men point to the perfect man, Jesus, who came to redeem fallen man. And that's the most important man we focus on here. Without Jesus' life of perfect obedience and without his death for our sins, we are helpless in our efforts to be better men. In fact, we are dead men walking, without hope and without purpose.

In the full context of God's creation of man and the redemptive work of Christ, we can now see numerous enduring lessons for manhood from Adam, Job, David, Solomon, and Paul. Among those lessons, the pages that follow spotlight the ones that are especially pertinent to the temptations and challenges of today's men.

Cultivating manhood for God's purposes
—

Applying the lessons that follow, in itself, does not constitute manhood, but living out those lessons can cultivate a rejection of passivity and the embrace of three essential characteristics of biblical manhood: leadership, provision, and protection.

This active cultivation is what prepares you for courageous engagement when your manhood is most needed. When David sought to explain to Saul why he was ready to go out and fight Goliath, he brought up past experiences that prepared him to take on this current fight (1 Sam 17:34-36). He had killed a lion and a bear and as a result knew he could kill Goliath.

You never know what Goliath moment(s) you were made for. Yours might be on the side of a road, in a coffee shop, in your living room, or even in a nicely decorated sanctuary. But you'll blow your moment or miss it altogether if you haven't cultivated biblical manhood.

Men who step up for God's purposes are rarely moving toward the need for the first time. They have cultivated instincts in situation after situation. They are tried and tested. They may have awkward moments, misunderstandings and setbacks in their efforts to engage, but they press on. Often the challenges they move toward disappear and the dangers they confront prove to be false alarms. But they learn from those experiences. They keep honing their instincts and continue to step forward versus stepping back.

God gives all of us opportunities each day to resist passivity and develop biblically masculine characteristics. Each of the challenges you face should be viewed as instruments in God's hands to help shape you — a masculine sanctification if you will. But remember this is not a self-reliant vision of masculinity. As a man, you are called to act, to lead, and work hard and at the same time, you are ultimately dependent on God.

David clearly understood that while he actively fought the lion and the bear, it was God who delivered him (1 Sam 17:37). As you cultivate manhood, recognize along with David that it is God who delivers and protects and cultivates. With that in mind, here are some ways you can, on a daily basis, cultivate masculine characteristics under the lordship of Christ.

ADAM
BIBLICAL LEADERSHIP

The LORD God took the man and put him
in the garden of Eden to work it and keep it. (Gen 2:15)

In *the Adventures of Huck Finn*, Huck colorfully describes an exchange with Jim, the escaped slave, that gets to the heart of our existence as men: "We had the sky up there, all speckled with stars, and we used to lay on our backs and look up at them, and discuss about whether they was made or only just happened. Jim allowed they was made, but I allowed they happened."

Manhood has everything to do with whether stars, and everything else in creation, "was made" or "only just happened." If Huck is right and it only just happened, then man is nothing more than lucky mud and everything in this book is just a vote for how men should evolve. If, however, Jim is right and "they was made," then we should seek the Maker.

That's the approach Jesus took in his exchange with the Pharisees: "Have you not read that he who created them from the beginning made them male and female, and said, 'Therefore a man shall leave his father and his mother and hold fast to his wife, and the two shall become one flesh'? (Matt 19:3-5). Later, the apostle Paul also directed believers back to the creation order in Genesis. And so we go back to the beginning and look at the first man, Adam, to find the origins of manhood.

As we read the story of Adam, we discover that God not only created the stars and mankind, but he created men with a specific direction and role. The first man demonstrates for us what our direction is as humans made in the image of God, but also what our specific roles are as men in that God-given direction.

The creation account in Genesis 1 reveals the shared work God gave men and women to do — he created mankind as male and female and tasked them both to take dominion, to subdue the earth and to be fruitful. The next two chapters of Genesis however, provide additional details about the creation of mankind, showing how men and women who are equal in essence are distinct in function in how they fulfill the tasks God gave them in a complementary way.

In the first three chapters of Genesis, we see that Adam is given the authority and responsibility to lead. God creates Adam first, creates Eve from Adam and for Adam, allows Adam to name the woman, calls the human race "man" after Adam, holds Adam morally responsible for eating the forbidden fruit even though Eve eats it first, and provides Adam with a suitable helpmate.

God's provision of Eve as a helpmate gives important context for how the tasks of Genesis 1 were to be fulfilled. After creating Adam from the dust, we read in Genesis 2:15, "The LORD God took the man and put him in the garden of Eden to work it and keep it." But then in verse 18, we read, "Then the LORD God said, "It is not good that the man should be alone; I will make him a helper fit for him." Eve is a helper perfectly suited for Adam, his complement who can come alongside him and help him exercise dominion, subdue the earth, and be fruitful.

The pattern and order of creation set in these chapters is for men to bear the authority and responsibility of leadership. And that hasn't changed. If you're a man, it's not optional to be a leader. It's your God-given assignment and identity. God calls you to lead in contexts throughout life.

The following are the five prototypical areas of leadership that come from the story of Adam:

Lessons in Manhood
—
Lead spiritually

"Where are you?" God asked Adam in the garden. Satan had gone to Eve and tempted her — usurping the authority structure God had put into place. But who did God go looking for? Adam. Why? God was holding Adam responsible for this family.

Adam should have been leading his wife. That was his God-given role and assignment and God held him responsible. What went down happened under Adam's watch and he was held to account. It's not that Adam and Eve weren't individually held accountable for their sin; they were. It's that Adam bore a distinct responsibility as the spiritual leader.

And that responsibility remains.

God held Adam accountable and he will hold you accountable. If you're married, you are responsible for your wife and children. You will answer for their spiritual condition.

If you're single, your job is to order your life and show self-mastery, to put disciplines in place and make provision for the day when you will have a wife.

Additionally, you have responsibility for the local church. Men are called to lead there with noble, humble leadership.

Men are to exercise spiritual leadership with maturity and good stewardship because we are going to be held accountable.

Lead in exercising dominion

God directed both men and women to take dominion and subdue the earth (Gen 1:26-30). Both men and women bring specific skills and inclinations, but God gave man a primary leadership responsibility in that work. He put Adam in the garden to work and keep it and then created Eve from Adam's side to be a "helper fit for him." It's at Adam's direction and under his leadership that the two co-labor to take dominion.

The task Adam had of working and keeping the garden had clear hands-on opportunities to take dominion. You may not have land to cultivate, but God has given you a domain somewhere. All of your leadership should demonstrate some aspect of taking dominion as you bring order and structure.

The exercising of dominion

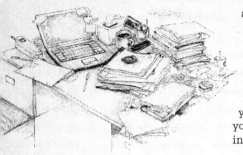

and keep it in order. Don't let your domains take dominion over you. A clean desk or organized garage doesn't constitute dominion, but it cultivates it and helps you take the same mindset to your family life, your work, and the world around you. How are you cultivating the inclination to order your world?

involves leadership and order. It's instinctive in men to order stuff. A man sees disorder (especially all the disorder that came once Adam sinned) and thinks — this shouldn't be. And so men order their lives, homes, families, and local church. This isn't dominance or dictatorship. It's responsibility.

God gives you opportunities to take dominion by giving you some area of domain — anywhere from a locker to a whole company. What domains has he given you? Even if a wife is helping you take dominion in those areas, how are you specifically leading and bearing responsibility?

What does your trunk, garage, closet, or desk look like? While most of us have a messy desk or car trunk on occasion, a life that is consistently characterized by disorder is evidence of a general pattern of passivity in the domains God gives you to work and keep. Your home, dorm room, garage, office, and car should bear the mark of your masculinity as you subdue it

Lead in production

God directed mankind to order and subdue, but also to produce. "Be fruitful and multiply" are his first words to man. God creates the earth, but he fills it with the means to continue the creation process. "Behold, I have given you every plant yielding seed that is on the face of all the earth, and every tree with seed in its fruit," he says. "You shall have them for food" (Gen 1:29).

In other words, God blesses mankind with the means and direction to be fruitful. The seeds provide a means for production. Adam and Eve produce that crop together and then prepare it to eat as the fuel to keep them productive. Adam and Eve also have within themselves the seed of life that allows them to be fruitful in having children. As they multiply, they have to be additionally productive to have the means to provide for their family.

Once again, this is a shared task. Men and women are both to be

> ## "Men bear the responsibility of providing — of knowing where provisions are going to come from."

fruitful and they each have a role in production, procreation, and provision.

Women have a significant role in procreation — as the bearers of life. "The man called his wife's name Eve," we read in Genesis 3, "because she was the mother of all living" (Gen 3:20). The means and motivation that a woman has to nurture her family plays a central part in her fruitfulness. It's a pattern throughout Scripture and evident in the Proverb of "the woman who fears the Lord" (Prov 31:10-31). This woman is incredibly fruitful as she cultivates and "works with willing hands" (Prov 31:13b). "She rises while it is yet night and provides food for her household" (Prov 31:15b).

But Adam has a leadership role to bear in production and provision. Remember Genesis 2:15: "The LORD God took the man and put him in the garden of Eden to work it and keep it." When Adam sinned, God frustrated the fruitfulness of his work, but still left him with that task: "By the sweat of your face you shall eat bread." And then we read, "[T]he LORD God sent him out from the garden of Eden to work the ground from which he was taken" (Gen 3:23).

Men still have to lead in provision. "[I]f anyone does not provide for his relatives, and especially for members of his household, he has denied the faith and is worse than an unbeliever" Paul wrote in 1 Timothy 5:8. Men bear the responsibility of providing — of knowing where the house payment, the groceries, and other provisions are going to come from.

Lead in establishing a family

God set a pattern with Adam of men taking the lead in forming new families. "It is not good that the man should be alone; I will make him a helper fit for him," God says in Genesis 2:18. And so God creates Eve from Adam's side. When God brings Eve to the man, Adam says: "This at last is bone of my bones and flesh of my flesh; she shall be called Woman, because she was taken out of Man" (Gen 2:23). And then God says, "Therefore a man shall leave his father and his mother and hold fast to his wife, and they shall become one flesh" (Gen 2:24).

What God communicates in this passage is: here's how I created the first family, I took some dust and I made a man and then I took part of his side and I made his wife. But in the future, a family will be established when a man leaves his father and mother and cleaves to his wife. This is the way it's going to be from now on. The man will take the initiative to leave his family and go create a new family. And men have to lead in the initiation because once they form a family, they are responsible to lead the whole thing.

If you don't feel gifted to sacrifice for the kingdom the joys of marriage, the pleasures of sex, and the blessing of children, then you should take the lead towards marriage. You should not wait on the sidelines for women to take the risks of approaching you. You should consider who in his sovereignty God has put around you and take on the risk of pursuing a suitable partner. And in your path to marriage, you should demonstrate the same sacrificial leadership that will be expected of you as a husband (Eph 5:23-31). That means taking the initiative to "leave father and mother" (Gen 2:24a), "find a wife" (Prov 18:22) "hold fast" to that wife as "one flesh" (Gen 2:24b) and then love her as Christ loves the church (Eph 5:31-33).

Lead in fighting the curse

The first two chapters of Genesis demonstrate the patterns and order of creation. But in Genesis 3, Adam and Eve fall and mankind is cursed along with the serpent. The work they were called to do remains, but the curse brings great challenge and frustration to that work.

The story of Adam's fall reveals three distinct areas where men have to be aware of the challenges of the curse:

STRUGGLE IN MARRIAGE

God tells Eve, "Your desire shall be for your husband, and he shall rule over you" (Gen 3:16b). God makes it clear how the curse will affect marriage — where one of the key and fundamental challenges will be. Some say that it's the curse that introduces gender roles in the home. But as we saw earlier, there was already a pattern of leadership before the fall. There's not a new relationship introduced here, just a new challenge.

The curse said that Eve was going to experience pain in childbirth, but God didn't say "now you're going to bear children." She already had the ability to be fruitful and have children, but because of the curse the bearing of children would be painful.

And God's not saying here that

as a result of the fall, there are now going to be gender roles and there's going to be authority and submission. That was already in place prior to the fall, He's just saying there are going to be increased challenges in this particular relationship. God is saying that men and women are going to have their most serious challenge here. It's going to boil down to conflict over these roles — who's leading and who's following.

Her temptation will be to usurp your authority and you'll struggle to get it back. You'll be tempted in your response to be either passive or domineering. If you're passive, you'll tempt her to further usurp authority and if you react in a domineering way, you could end up making her a doormat.

While God makes this challenge clear in an act of grace and mercy, churches often do their members a disservice by not dealing with this passage, because it makes them uncomfortable. But think about that. If you bought a car that had an oil leak, would you deal with it less or more? Would you say, "you know I don't like to talk about that leak, it just upsets me so much and I don't want to deal with it"? No. You know that the engine would just keep leaking and would eventually freeze up. You wouldn't ignore the problem if you had been specifically warned about it.

THORNS AND THISTLES
The next challenge is in the area of work: [T]o Adam he said:

> *"Because you have listened to the voice of your wife*
>   *and have eaten of the tree of which I commanded you,*
>   *'You shall not eat of it,' cursed is the ground because of you;*
>   *in pain you shall eat of it all the days of your life;*
>   *thorns and thistles it shall bring forth for you;*
>   *and you shall eat the plants of the field.*
>   *By the sweat of your face you shall eat bread,*
>   *till you return to the ground, for out of it you were taken;*
>   *for you are dust, and to dust you shall return."*
> *(Gen 3:17-19)*

Adam is now going to have to deal with thorns and thistles and till the ground by the sweat of his brow. God had already directed Adam to work, of course. It's just that now the relationship between Adam and the ground is going to be fraught with challenges and difficulties.

Even though we've developed pesticides, tractors, harvesters, and numerous other means for overcoming the curse over the years, we still have thorns and thistles in our work. Our work is still frustrating enough to require the sweat of our brow.

So, don't be surprised by the challenges you face in your work or in any effort to be productive and fruitful in life. Expect thorns and thistles. But keep working. Embrace the work God gives you without excuses. Don't grumble or complain.

EXTREMES IN LEADERSHIP

And finally, we see in the story of Adam two sinful temptations for men called to lead. First, we see in Adam's fall the temptation to abdicate leadership.

[T]he LORD God called to the man and said to him, "Where are you?" And he said, "I heard the sound of you in the garden, and I was afraid, because I was naked, and I hid myself." He said, "Who told you that you were naked? Have you eaten of the tree of which I commanded you not to eat?" The man said, "The woman whom you gave to be with me, she gave me fruit of the tree, and I ate." (Gen 3:9-12)

Adam abdicates his leadership role. When Eve sinned, he not only didn't intervene, he participated. Then he hid. He blamed. He did not lead. He was passive. Adam shifted from being Eve's protector to focusing on his own preservation.

The next thing we see in Adam's story is the temptation to abuse leadership. God told the woman, "Your desire shall be for your husband, and he shall rule over you" (Gen 3:16b). We looked earlier at how this added challenges to roles in marriage, but it also shows a temptation men face in all leadership roles — to rule over those they are supposed to serve. Instead of using their leadership to provide and protect, men are tempted to look down on those they lead, to be abusive and to use their authority to only care for themselves.

God has given you notice of where you'll have problems as a leader. You have to watch for those vulnerabilities and cultivate an instinct of engagement to overcome the temptation to either abdicate or abuse leadership.

Your leadership will now have challenges and temptations, but you still have to lead. ∞

JOB

SPIRITUAL RUGGEDNESS

"There was a man in the land of Uz whose name was Job, and that man was blameless and upright, one who feared God and turned away from evil." (Job 1:1)

The book of Job is deep, insightful, and ancient. It was the first book of the Bible — written over 4,000 years ago. The rough terrain of this book of wisdom brings us face to face with the reality of adversity and the need men have for Biblical ruggedness.

Job didn't have the spiritual armory men have available today: a Bible, a local church, a small group, a men's ministry, and yet he was widely known as a "blameless and upright man" — a reputation he maintained even in the face of tremendous and inexplicable suffering.

"Man who was born of a woman is few of days and full of trouble," Job observes (Job 14:1). It's inevitable that we will all suffer challenges and trials of some kind. There are a number of explanations in the Bible for why adversity is a common part of our lives. In the last section on Adam, we looked at how we now live in a fallen world. The fruit of a Genesis 3 world is sin, corruption, and difficulty. And we can't help but encounter the thorns and thistles of the fallen world even as people redeemed by Christ.

Another reason for why we face adversity is as a consequence of our individual sin — our troubles come from our own hands. Numbers 32:23 says, "be sure your sin will find you out." We overspend and deal with the consequences of debt. We break the law and pay the price. Often those consequences are orchestrated by God as a form of loving discipline for his children (see Heb 12:5-11). Paul tells us that God can also bring adversity to shape us for ministering to others who face trials (2 Cor 1:3-9) and to keep us from boasting in our own strength (2 Cor 12:6-10).

In Job we find that it's also possible to suffer for heavenly purposes with God choosing not to show us why. Job doesn't suffer because of something he has done wrong. In fact, we learn that Job is a blameless and upright man who consistently does things right. He remains for us a model leader in his faith, his work, his family, and his service to the needs of his community. The great extent of his suffering is a reminder that adversity in life is not always going to be proportionate to the good or evil things we do.

As readers of the book of Job, we discover something Job never know from his vantage point — that he was involved in a much larger cosmic battle. In Job 1:6-12, we see that Satan roams the earth as an accuser of the brethren (this insight is similar to what we read in 1 Peter 5:8 "Your adversary the devil prowls around like a roaring lion, seeking someone to devour"). We also see that God permits Satan to destroy the blessings Job has gained as a way to see if he has the character to still trust his maker.

In a single nightmarish day, Job faces the ultimate test. All the wealth and blessings he knows are tragically taken away one by one. Job experiences relentless, incessant adversity but remains steadfast. He is rugged enough in his character and trust in God to stand firm and to choose worship over complaint.

Job continues to be our model of

endurance as well as an insight into the sovereign care of God. He continues to inspire us today to be consistent in character and steadfast in trusting an unknown future to a sovereign known God.

Lessons in Manhood
—
Pay close attention to your character

Job had a coveted reputation. God describes him as blameless (Job 1:8). His moral character was without blemish. He was filled with integrity. He wasn't perfect. He was just a man, but the indication is that you couldn't lay a charge against him. There were no disqualifying flaws in his life. Everyone has a bad day, but there's a big difference between a bad day and a bad year — blowing it on occasion versus a pattern of serial moral failure and sinfulness. Job was not sinless, but he had a reputation as blameless.

God also characterizes Job as upright. In other words, he keeps in step with God. It's the word in Hebrew to describe cutting a straight path. Job stays on the straight and narrow. And what motivates him? The text of Job 1 goes on to say that it's because he fears God. He takes God seriously. Making the package complete is the reputation Job has for hating evil and turning away from it. He gets

out of the way of evil. He avoids the fruit of sin by staying away from the garden of sin.

God is at the epicenter of Job's life. His suffering, is not the result of sin, because Job is a strong model of spiritual character. In fact, Job's reputation for character is so strong that his wife, the person in his life who knew him best, affirms his reputation when she asks him in the face of all his suffering "do you still hold fast your integrity?" (Job 2:9).

Character is king. Job earned his from a life of consistency and integrity. What is your reputation for character? How would the people who know you best describe you? Do they know you for integrity?

Pay close attention to your character. "Keep a close watch on yourself," Paul tells Timothy (1 Tim 4:16). Remember that just as in the days of Job, Satan is roaming the earth as your accuser. You have to know your vulnerabilities, because Satan does.

Don't leave yourself vulnerable to Satan's slander. Live blameless and upright (Phil 1:10 and 2:25) in the righteousness of God (Rom 3:21-26). Fear God (2 Cor 7:1) and turn away from evil (Prov 3:7 and 1 Thess 5:22).

Serve the suffering

Job was a wealthy man. We read in Job 1:2 and 3, "There were

Decaf ☐
Shots ☐
Syrup ☐
Milk ☐
Donkey Milk ✓

When I went out to the gate of the city, when I prepared my seat in the square, the young men saw me and withdrew, and the aged rose and stood; the princes refrained from talking and laid their hand on their mouth; the voice of the nobles was hushed, and their tongue stuck to the roof of their mouth. (Job 7:10)

And why was that? Were they blown away by his wealth? That may have played into it, but as the text continues, we see that it had more to do with Job's character as an upright man:

When the ear heard, it called me blessed, and when the eye saw, it approved, because I delivered the poor who cried for help, and the fatherless who had none to help him. The blessing of him who was about to perish came upon me, and I caused the widow's heart to sing for joy. I put on righteousness, and it clothed me; my justice was like a robe and a turban. I was eyes to the blind and feet to the lame. I was a father to the needy, and I

born to him seven sons and three daughters. He possessed 7,000 sheep, 3,000 camels, 500 yoke of oxen, and 500 female donkeys, and very many servants, so that this man was the greatest of all the people of the east." Wealth in Job's day was measured in family and flocks. And Job was clearly blessed. From his livestock alone, he could have all the nice wool suits he wanted, plenty of transportation options, the finest cuts of meat and even the equivalent of unlimited Starbucks lattes — since warm donkey milk was considered a great delicacy in the land of Uz.

In chapter 29, we get a glimpse of Job in his prime:

*searched out the cause of
him whom I did not know.
I broke the fangs of the
unrighteous and made
him drop his prey from his
teeth. (Job 29: 11-17)*

This is an astounding model of bold, masculine servant leadership. Job didn't see the blessings of his life as a reason to lord over those around him. Instead, he served the poor, the fatherless, the dying, the widow, the blind, the lame, the needy, and those in need of justice.

This is what biblical manhood does. It serves needs and advocates for justice as the hands and feet of God. This informs how you can lead in serving the needs around you. The gifts and resources God has given you provide the means for you to serve others. Like Job, be diligent and masculine in your response to needs and in "breaking the fangs of the unrighteous" to free their prey.

Cover your home spiritually

Job was not only a man of high character who was a great success in business and the community, he was a also a dedicated family man. We read in verses 4 and 5:

*His sons used to go and
hold a feast in the house of
each one on his day, and
they would send and invite
their three sisters to eat
and drink with them. And
when the days of the feast
had run their course, Job
would send and consecrate
them, and he would rise
early in the morning
and offer burnt offerings
according to the number
of them all. For Job said, "It
may be that my children
have sinned, and cursed
God in their hearts." Thus
Job did continually.
(Job 1:4-5)*

Job, you can tell, was a dutiful dad. He got the job done as he made a priority of his family. His essential concern is for being the spiritual leader of his family. Even though Job didn't have the instruction of Deuteronomy 5 or Ephesians 6 for direction, he still showed great alertness and concern for the spiritual care of his family. Furthermore, Job offered sacrifices for his children even before the sacrificial system of the Levitical priesthood that started in the days of Moses.

And the text adds, "Thus did Job continually." This was a habit — not an occasional desperate prayer to God, but an ongoing commitment to intercede and sacrifice on behalf of his family.

Job is one of the earliest example

> "Adversity, after all, is what most distinctly reveals character. It exposes who you really are."

fathers have in the Bible for spiritual leadership in the family. From Job we learn: be alert spiritually, get up early and intercede on behalf of your family, and be continually faithful. Be engaged. Be a dutiful shepherd for your family. Parent from your knees. Beg God to intervene and protect your children's hearts so that they can be used mightily for his purposes.

Place your complete trust in God

Job's character was revealed in faithfulness to God, his community, and his family but it was more fully revealed when tragedy struck. Adversity, after all, is what most distinctly reveals character. It exposes who you really are.

In the rapid-fire verses of Job 1:13-19, we see the goodness and peace of Job's life tragically interrupted with news of an attack on his donkeys, oxen, and their attending servants. Before he can process that, another report comes of fire from the heavens destroying his sheep. And before he can get his mind around this double whammy, a follow-up report comes of an attack that wiped out his camels.

At this point, Job may have been thinking, at least I still have my family. But while the sole surviving servant from the camel attack was still speaking, another servant rushed in and told Job: "Your sons and daughters were eating and drinking wine in their oldest brother's house, and behold, a great wind came across the wilderness and struck the four corners of the house, and it fell upon the young people, and they are dead, and I alone have escaped to tell you" (Job 1:18-19).

How would you handle that?

Here's how Job responded: "Then Job arose and tore his robe and shaved his head and fell on the ground and worshiped" (Job 1:20). This is a primary difference between secular manhood and biblical manhood. As Job loses all his wealth and provision and then contemplates burying all ten of his children, there's no indication that he just stuffs his emotions and tries to act tough. Instead, he tears his robes as a sign of contrition, shaves his head to symbolize the glory departing from his life, and then

> ## "Will you be rugged enough to have unceasing, unconditional worship to God even if all the perks and success in life go away?"

falls on the ground ... and worships.

Satan had to be beside himself. He was sure Job would crack. He had said as much to God in verses 9 through 11: "Does Job fear God for no reason? Have you not put a hedge around him and his house and all that he has, on every side? You have blessed the work of his hands, and his possessions have increased in the land. But stretch out your hand and touch all that he has, and he will curse you to your face."

Satan was sure Job's faith wasn't robust enough to endure. He thought it was all a fraud because God was propping him up and that it would come crumbling down like a house of cards when crisis came.

But as all the heavens looked on in his moment of trial, Job responded to the worst kind of adversity in a way Satan could not have imagined. He not only didn't break, he showed contrition and worship. The person Satan thought to be weak was proved to be spiritually rugged.

Men today know what Job didn't know — that God was in control. We know even more about God's sovereignty in the context of the New Testament. In Paul's letter to the Romans, he writes, "And we know that for those who love God all things work together for good, for those who are called according to his purpose" (Rom 8:28). This is the insight we have as men today — God is in control and is working all things together for good if we are called according to his purpose.

Crisis will come in your life. It's not a matter of *if* you'll face a crisis but *when*. The day of trial will be what demonstrates your character. Will you be able to trust God and worship him in your day of trial? Will you be rugged enough to have unceasing, unconditional worship to God even if all the perks and success in life go away? Will you still place your full confidence in God?

Don't complain

All the disciplines of Job's life were for this moment. He was resolute and held fast under the ultimate pressure. What comes next in the text shows us the theology informing Job's ruggedness in the face of loss.

"And he said, 'Naked I came from my mother's womb, and naked shall I return. The Lord gave and the Lord has taken away. Blessed be the name of the Lord'" (Job 1:21).

Job knew great wealth in his life, but he remembered his roots. He entered life with nothing and knew he would leave with nothing. This is true of us all. Everything is on loan from the Lord: your money, your home, your career, your wife, your children, and your physical abilities. The Lord gives and he takes away. We set our affections on things above — not on things of this Earth (Col 3:1-2). Our response in all things should be to bless the name of the Lord.

That includes embracing God's hard gifts. We thank God for promotions, for spouses, for children, for food, for surprise gifts, but we also have to be willing to thank him for adversity. That's especially true when you consider how much more we know than Job did about God's plans in our suffering and trials. "We rejoice in our sufferings," Paul told the Romans, "knowing that suffering produces endurance, and endurance produces character, and character produces hope" (Rom 5:3-4). "Count it all joy, my brothers, when you meet trials of various kinds," wrote James, "for you know that the testing of your faith produces steadfastness" (Jas 1:2-3).

The final element of biblical ruggedness we see in the first chapter of the book of Job is this simple and yet man-sized last verse: "In all this, Job did not sin or charge God with wrong."

Few men today would blame Job for at least looking up to the heavens and asking, "Why God? Why me? I've done everything right. Why did all this happen to me?" But there's no complaining or questioning here. Job doesn't charge God with wrong.

Instead, by holding firm in his trust of God's wisdom, Job leaves a lasting legacy of endurance that is spotlighted in the New Testament. "Behold, we consider those blessed who remained steadfast," writes James, the brother of Jesus. "You have heard of the steadfastness of Job, and you have seen the purpose of the Lord, how the Lord is compassionate and merciful" (Jas 5:11).

Job's endurance was based on his hope of redemption: "For I know that my Redeemer lives," he says. "and at the last he will stand upon the earth. And after my skin has been thus destroyed, yet in my flesh I shall see God," (Job 19:25-26). ⚉

DAVID AND SOLOMON
"SHOW YOURSELF A MAN"

Be strong, and show yourself a man, and keep the charge of the LORD your God, walking in his ways and keeping his statutes, his commandments, his rules, and his testimonies, as it is written in the Law of Moses. (1 Kgs 2:2-3)

Much of the Bible speaks generally to men and women, but a message from King David to his son Solomon is distinctively masculine and fills in vital details on Biblical manhood.

1 Kings 2:1-9 records some of the last spoken words from a father

to his son. Here, David informs Solomon that death is near and he has important final instructions. He begins with an all-encompassing admonition that Solomon should show himself a man. In other words, he should demonstrate his manhood. He should do things that men are supposed to do. This is priceless and it gives a glimpse into David's understanding of what it means to be a man after God's own heart.

First David makes Solomon understand that manhood involves certain character. This means he is to demonstrate strength. The instruction is to "be strong." But this is not an individualistic, "pull yourself up by your bootstraps" type of strength. It is directly connected to Solomon's resolve to obey God.

David tells Solomon to "keep the charge of the Lord your God, walking in his ways and keeping his statutes, his commandments, his rules, and his testimonies, as it is written in the law of Moses …" (v. 3). David is reminding Solomon that God has spoken with regard to how one is to act and live. This is specifically concerning the laws of Moses. It includes not only the Ten Commandments and other instruction, but it involves the teaching about kings in Deuteronomy 17. In that passage, a king was told not to "acquire many horses for himself" (Deut 17: 16) or

to "acquire many wives," nor was he to amass "excess silver and gold" (Deut 17:17).

The next couple of verses in Deuteronomy 17 specifically required kings like Solomon to write out a personal copy of the law to keep close by for guidance.

David connects all of this to the covenant God made with him in 2 Samuel 7:12-16. God is going to establish the throne of his kingdom forever and David understands this covenant to be contingent upon the obedience of his offspring. David is underscoring for his son that manhood requires obedience to the one true and living God.

While manhood requires obedience to God, there is a particular context in which this will be worked out. In other words, the way in which Solomon is to work out his commitment to God will be particularly masculine. It is going to be in the context of leading, providing and protecting. In verses 5-9 Joab's unlawful killing of two of David's commanders is going to require a response from Solomon that involves avenging this act. Solomon is also going to have to protect and provide for the sons of Barzillai since they took care of David when he was running for Absalom. Finally he is instructed to arrange a bloody death for Shimei.

Imagine David giving last words to a daughter. He may very well

> "Challenges that can stretch you now prepare you for greater challenges later."

have included the first part of the instruction (obey the commands of God) but this second part would look very different. David's instruction has a particularly masculine context to it. Most of us know this intuitively. When there is a noise outside at night, men do not nudge their wife and say, "Honey, you go see what it is." Further, most of us would ridicule a man who did something like this. Biblical manhood is lived out in a particular manner, which means that while it has the same moral and spiritual constraints of biblical womanhood, it will many times look very different in its expression since it is seen most clearly in the role of leader, provider, and protector.

David's guidance to Solomon provides timeless detail for biblical manhood, but it also reminds us of the fallibility of men. David —

a man after God's own heart — transfers the throne to Solomon, who was the wisest king ever to live. Both leave behind a legacy for character and wisdom that still guides men today and yet they both fall dramatically short of God's standard.

The failures of David, Solomon, and the kings who followed them led the prophets to write of a king to come who would rule in righteousness. "Behold," writes the prophet Jeremiah, "the days are coming, declares the LORD, when I will raise up for David a righteous Branch, and he shall reign as king and deal wisely, and shall execute justice and righteousness in the land" (Jer 23:5).

Lessons in Manhood
—
Kill a lion or bear

Solomon grew up in the palace. His path to the throne was much smoother than the path his father David took. Like the sons of successful men who inherit their father's hard-earned wealth, Solomon was vulnerable to softness. There's no record of Solomon facing formative challenges that could prepare him for future challenges.

The instructions from David in 1 Kings 2:5-9 have immediate practical value, but they also provide Solomon with an opportunity to "kill a lion or bear." 1 Samuel 17 reminds us of the significance of David's life as a shepherd in preparation to fight Goliath:

> And Saul said to David, "You are not able to go against this Philistine to fight with him, for you are but a youth, and he has been a man of war from his youth." But David said to Saul, "Your servant used to keep sheep for his father. And when there came a lion, or a bear, and took a lamb from the flock, I went after him and struck him and delivered it out of his mouth. And if he arose against me, I caught him by his beard and struck him and killed him. Your servant has struck down both lions and bears, and this uncircumcised Philistine shall be like one of them, for he has defied the armies of the living God." And David said, "The LORD who delivered me from the paw of the lion and from the paw of the bear will deliver me from the hand of this Philistine." And Saul said to David, "Go, and the LORD be with you!" (1 Sam 17:33-37)

Challenges that can stretch you now prepare you for greater challenges later. God may have already brought challenges your way for this very purpose. If you haven't been stretched and cultivated for Goliath moments, however, there is value in seeking opportunities now to kill a lion or bear.

In other words, do something that is a challenge for you. That could mean actually killing a bear or a lion, but it could also mean a variety of other activities that require courage and stamina. It could be a health challenge such as running a marathon. Even challenges ranging from riding a roller coaster to snorkeling with sharks can help you cultivate instincts and confidence for future challenges.

A key benefit of taking on bold challenges is learning to press through even when your body might send you signals to flee danger. Whenever you take on a big challenge, your heart may beat fast as a sign of fear, but that doesn't mean you should run away. As John Wayne once said, "Courage is being scared to death, but saddling up anyway."

The real test of this cultivation is in making the shift from physical tests such as fighting a lion or bear into fighting the good fight of the faith (1 Tim 6:12). This could involve sharing the gospel with your lost friend or engaging the atheist at your workplace. It could mean signing up for a stretching missions project. Or it could mean finally dealing with a family conflict that you have allowed to go on for too long.

What lion or bear can you kill as a way to stretch you for future challenges?

Run to the battle/move toward the action

The instructions David gave Solomon required him to go right after pressing challenges and to initiate his kingdom with a pattern of moving toward the action. This was the pattern David had set over years of running to the battle and not being timid where manhood was needed.

Passivity is one of the main enemies of biblical masculinity and it's most obvious where it's needed most. It's a pattern of waiting on the sidelines until you're specifically asked to step in. Even worse than that, it can be a pattern of trying to duck out of responsibilities or to run away from challenges. Men who think conflict should be avoided, or who refuse to engage with those who would harm the body of Christ or their family, not only model passivity but fail in their responsibilities as protectors.

Running to the battle means routinely taking a step toward the challenge—not away from it. Instead of running and hiding, it means running into the burning building or into any other situation that requires courage and/or strength. It means having a burden of awareness and consistently asking yourself, "Is there any testosterone needed in this situation?" That doesn't mean being a fool who just rushes in, but simply being a leader with the instinct to go where the need is.

So show leadership, protection and provision in your family, work, church, and community by consistently moving toward the action. Demonstrate your availability by consistently asking those you encounter, "Do you need anything?" Watch for needs and challenges in whatever situation you're in and cultivate a habit of running to the battle.

Keep your head

Whether it was a bear attacking his sheep, Goliath looming in the distance, Saul hurling a spear at him or any other crisis David faced, he moved toward the action with calm resolve. He didn't panic. He was a man of action and engagement.

When there is a crisis, leaders don't panic. Crisis reveals character and capacity. This is the point when true leaders are distinguished from others.

So keep your head. Be anxious for nothing (Phil 4:6-7). Time is wasted while you panic. Just step forward.

Be unflappable and resilient.

Do the hardest task first

As he thought about becoming king, Solomon may have been looking forward to his coronation ceremony and other perks of leadership, but David made it clear that he had work to do first — and much of it would be hard and messy. But that's what leaders do. They ask, "what needs to be done?" and they get at it.

They are the first to roll up their sleeves. They volunteer for the hard work. They do the dirty jobs — the ones that are smelly and ugly — and they do their hardest work first.

As a matter of principle, procrastinating cultivates passivity. Attacking your hardest task of the day without delay will build your resistance to passivity. Waiting until the end of the day only reinforces your sinful tendencies toward passivity.

So lead with authority. The man who is cultivating biblical masculinity will not allow things like term papers, taxes, or project deadlines to rule him. He will exercise dominion over them by doing them in a timely manner. So do your work now rather than later.

But don't just be good with tasks, be bold with people. Make the hard relational move first, too. Don't be passive within interpersonal relationships. Some men are willing to do the hard task first, but avoid difficult situations that involve other people. Whether it means having a tough conversation, apologizing, or even exercising a Matthew 18:15-17-style confrontation, you should do your pain first.

Swear to your own hurt

Another lesson of David's instructions to Solomon (as well as the modeling of his life) is the importance of making and keeping commitments. In one of his Psalms, David writes, "Who shall sojourn in your tent? Who shall dwell on your holy hill?" (Ps 15:1). He responds: "He who walks blamelessly and does what is right and speaks truth in his heart," but then after a few more characteristics, he adds, "[He] who swears to his own hurt and does not change" (Ps 15:4b). That's a poetic way to say, "keep your commitments, even when it's inconvenient." David modeled this when Saul was aggressively seeking to kill him and yet David swore not to take the life of "God's anointed one" (1 Sam 24:1-22). After David became king, he extended kindness to the grandson of Saul (for the sake of Jonathan) even though that meant hosting a crippled man at the king's table for the rest of his life (2 Sam 9:1-13).

Men today struggle with commitments. David demonstrated leadership in both making and keeping commitments. Follow his example and you'll earn the trust of friends, employers, colleagues, church members, and your wife (or future wife). Don't show favoritism by bailing on people when you get a better offer. Don't throw in the towel when you've committed to a job or project. When it comes to a commitment, you only have two options: keep the commitment or renegotiate the commitment based on changes in circumstance (e.g. "I know I said I would be there to help you move this afternoon, but I got attacked by a mountain lion this morning, so I'll be a few minutes late").

See tasks through. Don't be known for starting and stopping projects. Carry stuff all the way through. Get it done. That's what leaders do. Swear to your own hurt and do not change.

Obey the Lord

The most enduring lesson of David and Solomon is the importance of obedience to the Lord. On the heels of saying, "Be strong, and show yourself a man," David adds, "and keep the charge of the LORD your God, walking in his ways and keeping his statutes, his commandments, his rules, and his

"Following God's design for biblical manhood can result in great rewards — relational happiness, business success, and personal fulfillment. But even if it doesn't, you still have to do it out of obedience."

testimonies" (1 Kgs 2:3). It would be through obedience that Solomon could be like his father, a man after God's own heart and available for his purposes.

David was clear in this message to Solomon. Strong, masculine leadership is tied to obedience. That means doing what God requires even if it doesn't seem to offer any practical benefits. "Sometimes it's not enough to do your best," Winston Churchill once said, "you have to do what's required."

Following God's design for biblical manhood can result in great rewards — relational happiness, business success, and personal fulfillment. But even if it doesn't, you still have to do it out of obedience. Obedience trumps tips and techniques. You can't just do the right things for what you can get out of it. In fact, you should obey the Lord's commands even if you end up like Joseph and your obedience brings you great trouble (Gen 39:1-20). Like Joseph, you obey and do the right thing even if it costs you everything.

Solomon, unfortunately does not faithfully obey God. Just a few chapters after the conversation between David and Solomon (in 1 Kgs 9-11) we learn that Solomon disobeys nearly every command Moses gave to kings in Deut. 17. He marries outside of the faith and

has to accommodate other worship practices (1 Kgs 9:24). He amasses horses and chariots for himself (10:26) and he acquires for himself excess silver and gold (10:21-22). He marries many women (11:1-3) and consequently, as Moses had warned, his heart is turned away toward other gods and he is not completely devoted to the Lord God of his father David (11:4-8).

A man after God's own heart doesn't just demonstrate leadership here and there; he faithfully loves God through obedience. "For this is the love of God," the apostle John writes, "that we keep his commandments. And his commandments are not burdensome" (1 John 5:3). ∞∞

"David and Solomon on Sex and Sin"

David committed adultery with Bethsheba. Solomon married foreign wives who turned him away toward foreign Gods. They both experienced the tragedy of being enticed by women and the subsequent tragedy of being distanced from God in the process.

Under the inspiration of the Holy Spirit, Solomon wrote a warning about sexual temptation and David recorded a prayer of repentance of his sexual sin. Both of these still guide men today.

FLEE SEXUAL TEMPTATION

Solomon's wisdom in Proverbs 5 offers a bold strategy for fighting lust — scriptures to aid you in resisting temptation.

1. My son, be attentive to my wisdom; incline your ear to my understanding,

2. that you may keep discretion, and your lips may guard knowledge.

   Be wise and have a pre-determined response to enticement.

3. For the lips of a forbidden woman drip honey, and her speech is smoother than oil,

4. but in the end she is bitter as wormwood, sharp as a two-edged sword.

5. Her feet go down to death; her steps follow the path to Sheol;

6. she does not ponder the path of life; her ways wander, and she does not know it.

   Unmask sin's beauty. Honey is sweet, but the bee stings.

7. And now, O sons, listen to me, and do not depart from the words of my mouth.

8. Keep your way far from her, and do not go near the door of her house,

   Don't depart from the truth. Don't put a question mark where God has put a period. Flee all known sources of

temptation. Make no provisions for the flesh. Recognize your vulnerabilities to sexual temptation — whether it's when you're traveling, when you're stressed, when you're tired, etc. And don't tolerate dabbling or just settle for sin management. Deploy extreme strategies to keep far from enticement. Consider the radical amputation recommended by Jesus on the Sermon on the Mount: "You have heard that it was said, 'You shall not commit adultery.' But I say to you that everyone who looks at a woman with lustful intent has already committed adultery with her in his heart. If your right eye causes you to sin, tear it out and throw it away. For it is better that you lose one of your members than that your whole body be thrown into hell. And if your right hand causes you to sin, cut it off and throw it away. For it is better that you lose one of your members than that your whole body go into hell. (Matt 5:27-30)*

9. lest you give your honor to others and your years to the merciless,
10. lest strangers take their fill of your strength, and your labors go to the house of a foreigner,
11. and at the end of your life you groan, when your flesh and body are consumed,
12. and you say, "How I hated discipline, and my heart despised reproof!
13. I did not listen to the voice of my teachers or incline my ear to my instructors.
14. I am at the brink of utter ruin in the assembled congregation.

"You may cover your sin, but God will uncover it.

Secret sin on earth is open scandal in heaven. One of the best things you can do is to write down 10 things you'd lose if you were caught doing something stupid — wife, family, reputation, education, home, job, etc. Use this reminder of consequences to shock your system.

Solomon goes on to show that your best defense is a strong offense:

15. Drink water from your own cistern flowing water from your own well.
16. Should your springs be scattered abroad, streams of water in the streets?
17. Let them be for yourself alone, and not for strangers with you.
18. Let your fountain be blessed, and rejoice in the wife of your youth,
19. a lovely deer, a graceful doe. Let her breasts fill you at all times with delight; be intoxicated always in her love.
20. Why should you be intoxicated, my son, with a forbidden woman and embrace the bosom of an adulteress?

    Be satisfied with your own marriage. A righteous marriage is your best alternative. If you are single, pursue becoming marryable.

    And, remember, we have an all-knowing, all-seeing God.

21. For a man's ways are before the eyes of the LORD, and he ponders all his paths.

    Ultimately, you're accountable for your sin.

22. The iniquities of the wicked ensnare him, and he is held fast in the cords of his sin.
23. He dies for lack of discipline, and because of his great folly he is led astray.

REPENT HUMBLY

If you've been enticed into sexual sin, repent and seek God's gracious forgiveness. "Repent therefore, and turn again, that your sins may be blotted out, that times of refreshing may come from the presence of the Lord" (Acts 3:19b-20a). King David's prayer following his adultery with Bathsheba still serves as a model of humble repentance:

Have mercy on me, O God, according to your
steadfast love; according to your abundant mercy
blot out my transgressions. Wash me thoroughly from
my iniquity, and cleanse me from my sin!

For I know my transgressions,
and my sin is ever before me.
Against you, you only, have I sinned
and done what is evil in your sight, so that you may
be justified in your words
and blameless in your judgment.
Behold, I was brought forth in iniquity,
and in sin did my mother conceive me.
Behold, you delight in truth in the inward being,
and you teach me wisdom in the secret heart.

Purge me with hyssop, and I shall be clean;
wash me, and I shall be whiter than snow.
Let me hear joy and gladness;
let the bones that you have broken rejoice. Hide your
face from my sins,
and blot out all my iniquities. Create in me a clean
heart, O God,
and renew a right spirit within me. Cast me
not away from your presence, and take not your
Holy Spirit from me. Restore to me the joy of your
salvation, and uphold me with a willing spirit.
(Ps 51:1-12)

JESUS

THE CRUX OF BIBLICAL MANHOOD

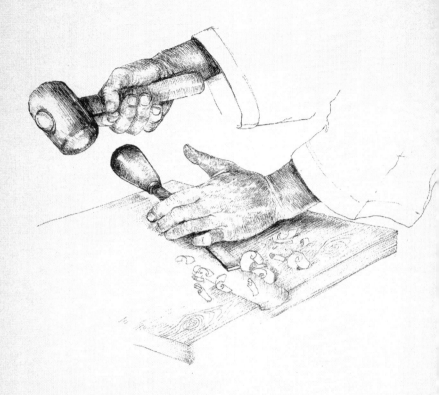

*For there is one God, and there is one mediator between God and men,
the man Christ Jesus. (1 Tim 2:5)*

Any study or pursuit of manhood is in vain if it overlooks the man of Jesus — for all our efforts to understand or live out our design as men culminate in Him. The crux of biblical manhood is in knowing who Jesus was as a man, what he came to do, why every man must wrestle with this man and what he calls us to as men today.

Who Jesus was as a man

Jesus lived as a man for us — not as a spirit, but as a man of flesh and blood. He was fully God but also fully man. We don't know a lot about what happened between the time Jesus was born and the period of his public ministry, but Luke reports on that period by saying, "And Jesus increased in wisdom and in stature and in favor with God and man" (Luke 2:52).

In other words, Jesus grew into manhood in the context of his wisdom, his physical capacities and his relationship with God as well as those around him. What we know about the life Jesus likely led at that time makes it impossible for Jesus to have been like some of the soft, delicate images we so often see of him today.

There's no sense that Nazareth was an effeminate or highly protected environment for Jewish boys when Jesus was young. Jesus most likely had thick forearms and strong scuffed hands from long hours of carpentry. He spent countless hours as an itinerant preacher on the dusty roads and rolling hills of Palestine under a hot sun that no doubt left him with leathery skin.

In truth, Jesus didn't look much different from the hard-working men around him. What distinguished him was how he acted as a man.

Since the fall of Adam, no one had ever seen a man live without sin. The world knew of men who did great things and yet those same men were known for doing evil. They knew men who were religious and pious and yet sinful in the midst of doing religious things.

Led by the Spirit and in obedience to the Father, Jesus lived out perfect manhood. He ate, drank, worked, rested, read, traveled, talked, listened, laughed, and cried — all without sin, but for the glory of God. He interacted with friends and family, rich and poor, pious and perverse, leaders and outcasts and engaged each one without pride, envy, respect of persons, contempt, or malice. Instead, he brought truth and love to each encounter in ways that often confounded those observing him.

What Jesus came to do

But Jesus wasn't just a good man who came to be an example. He spoke with authority — surpassing his teachers and religious leaders. He healed the sick, cast out demons, raised the dead, and calmed the storm.

"Where did this man get this wisdom and these mighty works?" people asked.

"The thief comes only to steal and kill and destroy. I came that they may have life and have it abundantly."
John 10:10

But there was a purpose behind his wisdom and mighty works. Again and again he proclaimed his purpose:

- "I must preach the good news of the kingdom of God to the other towns as well; for I was sent for this purpose" (Luke 4:43).
- "I have not spoken on my own authority, but the Father who sent me has himself given me a commandment — what to say and what to speak. And I know that his commandment is eternal life. What I say, therefore, I say as the Father has told me" (John 12:49-50).
- "The thief comes only to steal and kill and destroy. I came that they may have life and have it abundantly" (John 10:10).

- "[T]he Son of Man came not to be served but to serve, and to give his life as a ransom for many" (Matt 20:28).
- "[T]he Son of Man came to seek and to save the lost" (Luke 19:10).

And to his disciples he said plainly, "The Son of Man must suffer many things and be rejected by the elders and chief priests and scribes, and be killed, and on the third day be raised" (Luke 9:22). To that clear purpose, Jesus set his face like flint (Isa 50:7, Luke 9:51) and was undeterred in his path to the cross (Matt 16:21-23).

Just because his purpose was clear and because he was the Son of God, doesn't mean that it was easy. Remember, Jesus was made to be like us "in every respect" (Heb 2:17). His agony approaching the cross is clear in the account of his prayer in the garden before he was betrayed:

[Jesus] knelt down and prayed, saying, "Father, if you are willing, remove this cup from me. Nevertheless, not my will, but yours, be done." And there appeared to him an angel from heaven, strengthening him. And being in an agony he prayed more earnestly; and his sweat became like

*great drops of blood falling
down to the ground.
(Luke 22:41b-44)*

The agony and the blood flow steadily increased as Jesus was beaten, crowned with thorns, nailed to the cross and then pierced through the side.

He suffered like no other man, but "for the joy that was set before him endured the cross, despising the shame" (Heb 12:2).

How Jesus redeems fallen humanity

The men we've studied in this book each provide timeless insights and examples for us as men. We can model our lives on the lessons of purpose, leadership, resolve and initiative in their lives. But we see in each of these men flaws and gaps that leave them incomplete — that leave the accounts of their lives pointing to something else. Their stories are completed in the mission of Christ.

When we looked at Job earlier in this book, we only focused on the sorrows Job faced in chapter 1. In Job 2, we read about the second wave of sorrow dealt to Job that in a way points us to Christ:

*Again there was a day
when the sons of God
came to present themselves
before the LORD, and
Satan also came among
them to present himself
before the LORD. And
the LORD said to Satan,
"From where have you
come?" Satan answered
the LORD and said, "From
going to and fro on the
earth, and from walking
up and down on it." And
the LORD said to Satan,
"Have you considered my
servant Job, that there is
none like him on the earth,
a blameless and upright
man, who fears God and
turns away from evil? He
still holds fast his integrity,
although you incited me
against him to destroy
him without reason." Then
Satan answered the LORD
and said, "Skin for skin!
All that a man has he will
give for his life. But stretch
out your hand and touch
his bone and his flesh, and
he will curse you to your
face." And the LORD said
to Satan, "Behold, he is in
your hand; only spare his
life." (Job 2:1-6)*

God allowed Job, the "blameless and upright man," to face tremendous suffering and sorrow and yet he spared his life. When Jesus came and lived a perfect life, God allowed him not only to

> ## "Jesus was 'crushed for our iniquities.' In his great suffering as an innocent man, he bore our guilt."

suffer, but in fact he "did not spare his own Son" (Rom 8:32). Isaiah 53 tells us prophetically why God did not spare his Son, but instead allowed the sorrows, suffering and death of the cross:

> *Who has believed what he has heard from us? And to whom has the arm of the LORD been revealed?*
>
> *For he grew up before him like a young plant, and like a root out of dry ground; he had no form or majesty that we should look at him, and no beauty that we should desire him.*
>
> *He was despised and rejected by men; a man of sorrows, and acquainted with grief; and as one from whom men hide their faces he was despised, and we esteemed him not.*
>
> *Surely he has borne our griefs and carried our sorrows; yet we esteemed him stricken, smitten by God, and afflicted.*
>
> *But he was wounded for our transgression; he was crushed for our iniquities; upon him was the chastisement that brought us peace, and with his stripes we are healed.*
>
> *All we like sheep have gone astray; we have turned — every one — to his own way and the LORD has laid on him the iniquity of us all.*
> *(Isa 53:1-6)*

Jesus was "crushed for our iniquities." In his great suffering as an innocent man, he bore our guilt. We pointed out earlier that Job would make sacrifices on behalf of his children in case they had sinned. But in the book of Hebrews, we find that Jesus became the priest Job tried to be for his children:

*Since then we have a
great high priest who
has passed through the
heavens, Jesus, the Son of
God, let us hold fast our
confession. For we do not
have a high priest who is
unable to sympathize with
our weaknesses, but one
who in every respect has
been tempted as we are,
yet without sin.
(Heb 4:14-15)*

And yet Jesus was also the
sacrifice. He lived a perfect 33
years so that he might become
the perfect sacrifice for our sin:

*And every priest stands
daily at his service
offering repeatedly
the same sacrifices,
which can never take
away sins. But when
Christ had offered for
all time a single*

*sacrifice for sins, he
sat down at the right
hand of God, waiting
from that time until his
enemies should be made a
footstool for his feet.
(Heb 10:11-12)*

In that single sacrifice for our
sins, the apostle Paul explains that
Jesus became a second Adam:

*For as in Adam all die, so
also in Christ shall all be
made alive. (1 Cor 15:22)*

*Thus it is written, "The
first man Adam became
a living being"; the last
Adam became a life-giving
spirit. (1 Cor 15:45)*

In his resurrection, Jesus broke
the power of death that came
through Adam. Paul explains this
more in 1 Corinthians:

*For I delivered to you as
of first importance what I
also received: that Christ
died for our sins in
accordance with the
Scriptures, that he was
buried, that he was
raised on the third
day in accordance
with the Scriptures ...
And if Christ has not
been raised, then our*

preaching is in vain and your faith is in vain. ... The sting of death is sin, and the power of sin is the law. But thanks be to God, who gives us the victory through our Lord Jesus Christ.
(1 Cor 15:3-4, 14, 56-57)

The life, death, and resurrection of Jesus also inaugurated a kingdom that fulfilled what began with King David, but far surpassed what David or Solomon or any king who followed them could do as sinful men. Speaking in Antioch, Paul makes the connection: "[God] raised up David to be their king, of whom he testified and said, 'I have found in David the son of Jesse a man after my heart, who will do all my will.' Of this man's offspring God has brought to Israel a Savior, Jesus, as he promised" (Acts 13:22-23).

So Jesus, the root of David (Rev 22:16), lived the life of perfect obedience that David and Solomon never could in order to make us righteous (Rom 5:18-19) and to provide us entrance into an eternal kingdom (2 Pet 1:3-11).

Jesus rules today as king, preparing for the full consummation of the Kingdom of God. "Then comes the end," Paul writes, "when [Jesus] delivers the kingdom to God the Father

> "Jesus was the hinge of redemption history. He paid the price to redeem us as men and women."

after destroying every rule and every authority and power. For he must reign until he has put all his enemies under his feet" (I Cor 15:24).

While he was on the Isle of Patmos, the apostle John got a divine glimpse of that consummation — the final completed mission of Christ:

Then I saw heaven opened, and behold, a white horse! The one sitting on it is called Faithful and True, and in righteousness he judges and makes war. His eyes are like a flame of fire, and on his head are many diadems, and

*he has a name written
that no one knows but
himself. He is clothed in
a robe dipped in blood,
and the name by which
he is called is The Word
of God. And the armies of
heaven, arrayed in fine
linen, white and pure,
were following him on
white horses. From his
mouth comes a sharp
sword with which to
strike down the nations,
and he will rule them
with a rod of iron. He will
tread the winepress of the
fury of the wrath of God
the Almighty. On his robe
and on his thigh he has
a name written, King of
kings and Lord of lords.
(Rev 19:11-16)*

Every man has to wrestle with this Man

Jesus was the hinge of redemption history. He paid the price to redeem us as men and women. He bore the punishment on the cross for our darkest sins and offers to exchange his righteousness for our unrighteousness. It's our prayer that if you have not been born again (John 3:1-16), that the Holy Spirit will use the means of this book to proclaim the truth that brings new life in Christ:

*[I]f you confess with
your mouth that Jesus is
Lord and believe in your
heart that God raised him
from the dead, you will
be saved. For with the
heart one believes and is
justified, and with the
mouth one confesses and
is saved. (Rom 10:9-10)*

What we do with the life and sacrifice of Jesus is life's ultimate question and our only hope for eternal life. "For there is one God," Paul writes, "and there is one mediator between God and men, the man Christ Jesus" (1 Tim 2:5). All men are going to have to answer to Jesus. The gospel makes it clear that there is a future appointment for each of us to stand before Christ (Heb 9:27).

When the God of the universe takes on the form of man we are compelled to take notice, repent of indwelling sin, submit to his lordship and seek refuge in the only man that can save us from our sins. Reckoning with Jesus is the first act in redeeming masculinity. He is the epitome and example of biblical manhood and without him we will only distort our God-given identity and role. It's our unapologetic desire that you come face-to-face with the one man who can redeem your

> "What we do with the life and sacrifice of Jesus is life's ultimate question and our only hope for eternal life."

masculinity from distortion and transform your life for his glory.

What Jesus calls us to as men today

Just before he was crucified, Jesus, filled with authority and power, set an example for us all:

> Jesus, knowing that the Father had given all things into his hands, and that he had come from God and was going back to God, rose from supper. He laid aside his outer garments, and taking a towel, tied it around his waist. Then he poured water into a basin and began to wash the disciples' feet and to wipe them with the towel that was wrapped around him. (John 13:3-5)

The disciples didn't expect Jesus to take on the lowly task of washing their feet of the grime, manure and muck they would have been covered with from the roads they had walked. And they weren't expecting Jesus to then call them to lead in the same way:

> When he had washed their feet and put on his outer garments and resumed his place, he said to them, "Do you understand what I have done to you? You call me Teacher and Lord, and you are right, for so I am. If I then, your Lord and Teacher, have washed your feet, you also ought to wash one another's feet. For I have given you an example, that you also should do just as I have done to you. Truly, truly, I say to you, a servant is not greater than his master, nor is a messenger greater than the one who sent him. (John 13:12-16)

In this act and commission, Jesus clearly connected for his disciples what he had faithfully lived throughout his life: servant leadership, strength and humility. Jesus exceeded in his life all the

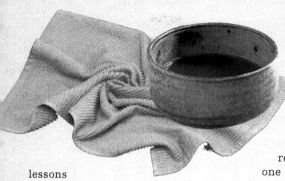

commanded you. And behold, I am with you always, to the end of the age." (Matt 28:18-20)

This final direction gave the apostles a clear mission for the rest of their lives and one that has passed down through the centuries until it has become our mission today.

As men redeemed by the blood of Christ, empowered with the Holy Spirit, trained by the teaching and servant leadership of Jesus, and commissioned with the gospel, the apostles were changed men. Men like Peter who had been overly aggressive in his manhood (Matt 16:23 and John 18:10) and also cowardly in the moment of trial (Matt 26:69-75), grew to be bold in ministry (Acts 4:13), but also tender and servant-hearted (1 Pet 3:8-9, and 5:1-3, 6).

lessons of Adam, Job, David, and Solomon — bringing completion to their stories as the perfect man they could never be. But in washing the feet of his disciples, and then giving his life on the cross, he also redefined the context of biblical manhood and leadership as sacrificial and servant-hearted.

After his resurrection, Jesus directed his apostles to a mountain in Galilee where he gave them a final commission:

And Jesus came and said to them, "All authority in heaven and on earth has been given to me. Go therefore and make disciples of all nations, baptizing them in the name of the Father and of the Son and of the Holy Spirit, teaching them to observe all that I have

The lives of the disciples as well as the other gospel-driven men we read about in the New Testament (such as Luke, Stephen, Paul, Timothy, and more) show us what kind of men Jesus calls and empowers us to be today — redeemed, Spirit-led, fighting the good fight, following hard after Christ, and ready to go where he sends us for the gospel. ∞

PAUL

Grace and grit for the gospel

Be watchful, stand firm in the faith, act like men, be strong. Let all that you do be done in love. (1 Cor 16:13-14)

Last words are important. As the Apostle Paul wraps up the letter that becomes 1 Corinthians, there's an urgency in his message. He's addressed a lot of messiness in the church of Corinth and now he's going to specifically call out the men of the church for their role moving forward: "Be watchful, stand firm in the faith, act like men, be strong. Let all that you do be done in love" (1 Cor 16:13-14).

In clear, rapid-fire staccato, Paul gives five imperatives — not electives or options, but divine mandates. His words are exhortive in nature, with the intention of grabbing hold of his readers and calling them to step up as men.

They are written by a man whose life has been radically altered by Jesus Christ and who is now fully expending his manhood for the sake of the gospel.

Based on Paul's understanding that our ultimate fight is "against the spiritual forces of evil in the heavenly places" (Eph 6:12), we shouldn't be surprised to see that four of the five imperatives he gives to the men of Corinth are military metaphors. He's stressing a wartime mindset and calling for galvanized men for the gospel.

Throughout the Old Testament, God speaks through patriarchs, kings, prophets and poets and tells men to "watch," "stand firm," and "be strong." His words give his chosen people the ability to face daunting armies, walled cities and other dire circumstances. Paul echoes these words for the men of Corinth in the context of their present practical and spiritual challenges. His words, in fact, are very similar to those David spoke to Solomon from his death bed: "Be strong, and show yourself a man, and keep the charge of the LORD your God" (1 Kgs 1:2b-3a).

With his charge, Paul demonstrates the need for men to continue to watch, be strong, act like men, and stand firm, but he adds the gospel imperative to do it all in the context of love. He affirms the need to be strong and resolved, but also to be redeemed by grace. His call to grit and grace keeps men from the extremes of either abdicating or abusing leadership. It galvanizes men to be strong and humble leaders.

In that context, we see Paul's message as containing five convictions of New Testament leadership — empowered by the cross and deployed for the sake of the gospel.

LESSONS IN MANHOOD
—

Be watchful

Paul starts by urging men to pay attention, to be on the alert. The word he uses appears 22 times in the New Testament. It means to be watchful, awake, vigilant, and discerning. It's most often used concerning the coming of Christ — stressing the need to be ready for his return. But it's also used in the context of being watchful because of the reality of our spiritual enemy — and that's the context here. You have to be alert, sober, and awake because you have a determined enemy.

God has a plan for your life, but so does Satan. In John 10:10, we see that Jesus came to give us life while the thief comes only to "steal, kill and destroy." The apostle Peter stresses watchfulness in a description of Satan that is even more ominous: "Be sober-minded; be watchful," he writes. "Your adversary the devil prowls around like a roaring lion, seeking someone to devour" (1 Pet 5:8).

Leaders have to be aware. You have to get up in the morning, put your feet on the floor, put your toes toward the door and immediately meditate on the gospel with the theological understanding that you're being hunted. Satan is hunting you personally. You are prey — the food of choice — for the devil.

You can understand this best watching a documentary about lions and other hunters of the wild. Lions go after the weakest members of the herd. They let their prey get comfortable with their presence while they move in closer for the kill. The day you stop running, you'll be devoured. You need to be watchful to know where you're vulnerable, because Satan does. You are a flawed man and a flawed leader and the enemy will attack there. Your pride? He'd just as soon flatter as roar. Your purity? He'd just as soon put on a dress as look beastly.

You can't let your guard down. You can't get spiritually lazy. To use another biblical metaphor, you are like a watchman on the wall (Isa

21:6-8), and you have to know where the city is weak. You have to know your surroundings and compensate for your vulnerabilities. It could be:

- when you're tired — when your guard is down because you're weary.
- when you're traveling — and feel anonymous in a different place where you think you can do things that you couldn't do back home where you have a community of accountability you're used to.
- or when you're under trial — when the pressure is on and you're tempted to look for an escape.

It's at your point of vulnerability that you raise your alert, when you get your game on, when you have to be at full capacity in your watchfulness. You have to be intentional. If you don't attack life, life will attack you. You have to go on the offense. You need self-mastery. Your leadership starts with self-control. You can't lead others until you lead yourself.

Be watchful so you can see things coming and then get far away from sin. As Paul says in Romans 13:14, "make no provision for the flesh, to gratify its desires." Don't let yourself be in proximity to sin. Don't expose yourself. Being watchful means being an alert man:

knowing the threat and ordering your life appropriately.

Stand firm in the faith

The next charge is to stand firm. A common theme of leadership is the need to be steadfast and stable. Be resolute, especially in your convictions. Plant your feet shoulder length apart so that you can't be easily blown off course.

But stand firm in the faith. Stand on what is solid (Matt 7:24-27). Take a stand on the rock of absolute truth in a sandy world without absolutes.

To stand firm in the faith you have to know the faith. You have to be grounded in the Scriptures. You have to be truth-driven, Scripture-soaked and washed. You have to know and articulate the gospel. You're only able to stand firm and

put off the fear of man when you are informed by the fear of God.

You need a dogged tenacity, a voraciousness for the truth of the Word of God marked by a red-hot devotional life. Ransack your Bible, tear through it with urgency and let it work your soul out and work into the DNA of who you are. You need that spiritual stability.

Remember how Jesus responded when he was tempted by Satan — he went to Scripture. Again and again he said, "It is written..." To stand firm in the faith, you have be able to call on Scripture when you're under attack.

Think of it in the context of hand to hand combat in the military. When you're standing firm, you're able to take a punch. You've got your dukes up. You're alert and watching.

You're dodging and weaving. You're steady and able to fight. That's the picture Paul's giving. In his letter to the Ephesians, he adds the context of doing this in the "whole armor of God": "Therefore take up the whole armor of God," he writes, "that you may be able to withstand in the evil day, and having done all, to stand firm" (Eph 6:13).

Act like men

At this point, Paul appeals to the brothers at Corinth to act like men. His call is not like popular concepts today of manning up or bucking up. Paul is calling the men of Corinth to act mature. In other words, act like adults, grown-ups. Put away childish thinking and behavior. Stop the silliness and the nonsense.

It's the word we so often need to hear from older men in our lives — men who can, in love, put their arm around us and call us out. We need older men who take Titus 2 seriously and find opportunities to say, "you need to act like a man — you're acting like a boy." Manhood requires being able to give and receive that kind of constructive criticism.

As you hear that charge from Paul, where do you need most to mature? Where are you failing to engage in your God-given assignment and identity?

Perform like a man. Step up and lead.

Be strong

Once again, Paul's words to the Corinthians echo David's words to Solomon: "be strong."

Be level-headed, unflappable and tough. Do the hard things. Take risks. Cultivate thick skin. Get in the battle. Be willing to fight and take some shots, to be criticized, and even to have enemies ("You have enemies?" Winston Churchill asked, "Good. That means you've stood up for something, sometime in your life.")

The great power in Paul's words, however, come from an alternative translation of the Greek that renders the phrase: "be strengthened". In other words, don't rely on your own strength, rely on Christ. In the context of Philippians 4:13, move beyond macho weight-pumping strength to the grace-induced, spirit-filled, Christ-resolved, gospel-driven strength to lead.

This is the quiet resolve and tenacity of New Testament leadership that strengthens men to lead. It's what was needed in the Corinthian church and it's what's needed in your local church:

- **It's the strength to do the heavy lifting.** To get dirty, to show up and do the hard work.
- **It's the strength to do more than just play it safe.** Safety is mediocrity and God hates mediocrity (Revelation 3:16).

"Be strengthened by the giver of strength"

- **It's the strength to work to the point of exhaustion.** "The world is run by tired men," observed Oswald Sanders, not by men looking for easy street or unwilling to engage. And this is especially true in the local church. Look closely and you'll see men who are working hard doing the heavy lifting of the gospel.

- **It's the strength to seek not a title, but a labor.** Notice the language in 1 Timothy 3: "If anyone aspires to the office of overseer, he desires a noble task." Spiritual leaders, strengthened by God don't desire titles, they desire tasks. If you have a title in a local church, but don't have God-empowered character, thick skin, tenacity and humility, you're not going to have the strength to do your noble task.

"If you have raced with men on foot, and they have wearied you, how will you compete with horses?" writes the prophet Jeremiah, "And if in a safe land you are so trusting, what will you do in the thicket of the Jordan?" (Jer 12:5).

Strength is essential for the tasks men are called to do and the challenges they will face, so be strengthened by the giver of strength:

> Have you not known? Have you not heard? The LORD is the everlasting God, the Creator of the ends of the earth.
> He does not faint or grow weary; his understanding is unsearchable.
> He gives power to the faint, and to him who has no might he increases strength.
> Even youths shall faint and be weary, and young men shall fall exhausted; but they who wait for the LORD shall renew their strength; they shall mount up with wings like eagles; they shall run and not be weary; they shall walk and not faint.
> (Isa 40:28-31)

Let all you do be done in love

Finally, Paul completes his charge with the essential context of love. He says, "do everything in love." Without love and passion, the previous four entries will just be fleshly, abrasive, and harsh. Be firm, but not hard. God isn't calling you to be a hard, macho leader. He's calling you to have humility and

> ## "The most attractive and effective element of your leadership will be your love."

strength perfectly blended together. Tenacity and tenderness. Gospel leadership isn't hard and abrasive, it's compassionate and gracious.

Look at the context for love that Paul reveals earlier in his letter to the Corinthians:

> *If I speak in the tongues of men and of angels, but have not love, I am a noisy gong or a clanging cymbal. And if I have prophetic powers, and understand all mysteries and all knowledge, and if I have all faith, so as to remove mountains, but have not love, I am nothing. If I give away all I have, and if I deliver up my body to be burned, but have not love, I gain nothing. (1 Cor 13:1-3)*

The whole package matters to Paul. You can't just have some of the pieces, it all has to be there.

The most attractive and effective element of your leadership will be your love. As you lead in your home, your church and the marketplace, you need skill for the work at hand, conviction to stand on truth and righteousness with integrity and courage to do the right thing, but you especially need the humility, kindness and grace that come from doing all things in love.

It's based on the new commandment Jesus gave at the Last Supper: "A new commandment I give to you, that you love one another: just as I have loved you, you also are to love one another. By this all people will know that you are my disciples, if you have love for one another" (John 13:34-35).

"[B]e imitators of God, as beloved children," Paul wrote to the church in Ephesus, "And walk in love, as Christ loved us and gave himself up for us, a fragrant offering and sacrifice to God" (Eph 5:1).

This is the depth of the love and passion that marks out New Testament and biblical leadership: selfless sacrifice, up to the point of physically laying your life down for others. And this is what what it means for you as a man to lead with that kind of love:

Lead from the position of humility: Just before commanding his disciples to love others, Jesus demonstrated his love by washing their feet (see John 13:1-16). He led them by taking on the role of a lowly servant. Manhood is not about taking and leading for your own gain. It's about serving.

Put others ahead of yourself: In his letter to the Philippians, Paul demonstrated the full extent of Christ's life as a servant:

> Have this mind among yourselves, which is yours in Christ Jesus, who, though he was in the form of God, did not count equality with God a thing to be grasped, but made himself nothing, taking the form of a servant, being born in the likeness of men. And being found in human form, he humbled himself by becoming obedient to the point of death, even death on a cross. (Phil 2:5-8)

In this light, Paul charges the Philippians:

> Do nothing from rivalry or conceit, but in humility count others more significant than yourselves. Let each of you look not only to his own interests, but also to the interests of others. (Phil 2:3-4)

In the example and power of Christ, you should esteem others. Look out for others. Don't take credit from others — applaud them, or as Paul says to the Romans, "Out do one another in showing honor" (Rom 12:10). Say *no* to yourself and *yes* to others.

God honors humility, but opposes the proud (Jas 4:6).

Love people instead of things: The smallest package in the world is a man wrapped up in himself observed Benjamin Franklin. The legacy of your life will be shallow if it's centered on you and your stuff. It's also a poor investment.

> "Do not lay up for yourselves treasures on earth, where moth and rust destroy and where thieves break in and steal," Jesus warned in the Sermon on the Mount, "but lay up for yourselves treasures in heaven, where neither moth nor rust destroys and where thieves do not break in and steal. For where your treasure is, there your heart will be also."
> (Matt 6:19-21)

What really matters are the people God gives you the opportunity to love. "For the whole law is fulfilled in one word," Paul tells the Galatians, "You shall love your neighbor as yourself" (Gal 5:14).

Your orientation has to be to love people and use things — not the other way around. Have a soft heart for the people in your family, neighborhood, church, and workplace. Let your heart be broken by the suffering people around you, especially those who are headed toward eternal suffering. ◙

Cultivate spiritual allies

One of the most significant things you learn from the life of Paul is that the self-made man is incomplete. Paul believed that mature manhood was forged in the body of Christ. In his letters, Paul talks often about the people he was serving and being served by in the body of Christ. As you live in the body of Christ, you should be intentional about cultivating at least three key relationships based on Paul's example:

1. **Paul:** *You need a mentor, a coach, or shepherd who is further along in their walk with Christ.* You need the accountability and counsel of more mature men. Unfortunately, this is often easier said than done. Typically there's more demand than supply for mentors. Some churches try to meet this need with complicated mentoring matchmaker type programs. Typically, you can find a mentor more naturally than that. Think of who is already in your life. Is there an elder, a pastor, a professor, a businessman, or other person that you already respect? Seek that man out; let him know that you respect the way he lives his life and ask if you can take him out for coffee or lunch to ask him some questions — and then see where it goes from there. Don't be surprised if that one person isn't able to mentor you in everything. While he may be a great spiritual mentor, you may need other mentors in the areas of marriage, fathering, money, and so on.

2. **Timothy:** *You need to be a Paul to another man (or men).* God calls us to make disciples (Matt 28:19). The books of 1 and 2 Timothy demonstrate some of the investment that Paul made in Timothy as a younger brother (and rising leader) in the faith. It's your job to reproduce in others the things you learn from the Paul(s) in your life. This kind of relationship should also be organic. You don't need to approach strangers to offer your mentoring services. As you lead and serve in your spheres of influence, you'll attract other men who want your input. Don't be surprised if they don't quite know what to ask of you. One practical way to engage with someone who asks for your input is to suggest that they come up with three questions that you can answer over coffee or lunch and then see where it goes from there.

3. **Barnabas:** *You need a go-to friend who is a peer.* One of Paul's most faithful ministry companions was named Barnabas. Acts 4:36 tells us that Barnabas's name means "son of encouragement." Have you found an encouraging companion in your walk with Christ? Don't take that friendship for granted. Enjoy the blessing of friendship, of someone to walk through life with. Make it a priority to build each other up in the faith. Be a source of sharpening iron (Prov 27:17) and friendly wounds (Prov 27:6) for each other. But also look for ways to work together to be disruptive — in the good sense of that word. Challenge each other in breaking the patterns of the world around you in order to interrupt it with the gospel. Consider all the risky situations Paul and Barnabas got themselves into and ask each other, "what are we doing that's risky for the gospel?"

A
—
GUIDE
—
FOR
—
HUSBANDS

Ephesians 5:22-33

Wives, submit to your own husbands, as to the Lord. For the husband is the head of the wife even as Christ is the head of the church, his body, and is himself its Savior. Now as the church submits to Christ, so also wives should submit in everything to their husbands.

Husbands, love your wives, as Christ loved the church and gave himself up for her, that he might sanctify her, having cleansed her by the washing of water with the word, so that he might present the church to himself in splendor, without spot or wrinkle or any such thing, that she might be holy and without blemish. In the same way husbands should love their wives as their own bodies. He who loves his wife loves himself. For no one ever hated his own flesh, but nourishes and cherishes it, just as Christ does the church, because we are members of his body. "Therefore a man shall leave his father and mother and hold fast to his wife, and the two shall become one flesh." This mystery is profound, and I am saying that it refers to Christ and the church. However, let each one of you love his wife as himself, and let the wife see that she respects her husband.

Colossians 3:19

Husbands, love your wives, and do not be harsh with them.

I Peter 3:7

Likewise, husbands, live with your wives in an understanding way, showing honor to the woman as the weaker vessel, since they are heirs with you of the grace of life, so that your prayers may not be hindered.

Lead in Love

Even the least observant men among us know that they should love their wives. That's clear in the passages included here from the writings of Peter and Paul. But, when you look at the context of their writing, you see that there's a particular way men are to love their wives.

Men are to lead in love.

In his letter to the Ephesians, Paul writes, "Wives, submit to your own husbands, as to the Lord. For the husband is the head of the wife even as Christ is the head of the church, his body, and is himself its Savior" (Eph 5:22-23). Far from saying that authority and submission are a bad thing in marriage, Paul is saying that they're supposed to be there and it's supposed to picture Christ in the church, but he goes on to explain that it's to be done in a particular way.

He writes, "In the same way husbands should love their wives as their own bodies. He who loves his wife loves himself. For no one ever hated his own flesh, but nourishes and cherishes it, just as Christ does the church, because we are members of his body" (Eph 5:28-30).

So there's a picture of the Gospel here — a particular way to lead in love. You're supposed to do it as if it were second nature, just like how you care for your own body. It's very natural for you to drink something when you get thirsty or to eat something when you get hungry or to go to the doctor if you get sick or injured. Nobody gives you an award for that. That's just how you treat your own body. Now that

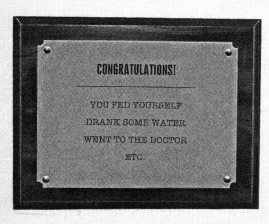

CONGRATULATIONS!

YOU FED YOURSELF
DRANK SOME WATER
WENT TO THE DOCTOR
ETC.

"Leadership should be to the point of your own self-neglect"

you're "one flesh" with your wife in marriage, you're to lead in such a way as if you were naturally caring for your own body.

Later, Paul writes to the Colossians, "Husbands, love your wives, and do not be harsh with them" (Col 3:19). Now, why would he say that? Maybe he's anticipating under the influence of the Holy Spirit that in a fallen world, there may be certain sinful tendencies a man might have to be harsh with his wife instead of being gentle like he should. It's the same reason that Paul warns us not to think more highly of ourselves than we ought to think (Rom 12:3). Why? Because we tend to do that.

When the apostle Peter writes about marriage he says, "husbands live with your wives in an understanding way, showing honor to the woman as a weaker vessel, since they are heirs with you of the grace of life" (1 Pet 3:7a). Why would Peter need to remind husbands that their wives are heirs with them — that they are equal to them? Because, in a fallen world, people who are given authority sometimes believe that they are better than the people they're leading. In a marriage, a man in his sinfulness can be deluded into thinking that because he's the leader, he's better. And so Peter reminds husbands to treat their wives as equals.

When Adam saw Eve for the first time, he said, "this is bone of my bone, flesh of my flesh" — he was saying, you're equal to me, you're the same substance as me. In Galatians 3:28, Paul helps us understand our equality in Christ: "There is neither Jew nor Greek, there is neither slave nor free, there is no male and female, for you are all one in Christ Jesus." Paul isn't saying, "in Christ you lose your ethnicity, your job status or your gender," but he is saying that those things don't give you additional status with God — it's Christ alone.

God gives us authority and leadership as men, but it's not to be used for our own self-aggrandizement; it's to be used for the good of those we're serving. That's why we call it servant leadership and sacrificial leadership. It should be to the point of your own self-neglect; for the good of those you're leading.

So what does it look like to daily lead in love? Much could be offered here, but we want to focus on five practical ways that men should lead their marriages in love.

Race to repentance and forgiveness

In a Genesis 3 world, your marriage depends on forgiveness and repentance. James says we all stumble in many ways (Jas 3:2) and that means you and your wife will stumble ... in many ways. You can't be surprised when your wife sins, you just have to be committed to live out the "or worse" part of your vows and be ready to forgive.

James adds later that we should confess our sins to one another and pray for one another (Jas 5:16). That means you can't be defensive — you need to confess your sin and repent (turn away from it). As the leader in your marriage, you should, in fact, be the first to repent and the first to forgive. If someone needs to own something in the home, it should be you.

In his letter to the Ephesians, Paul provides a general message for the body of Christ that you have the opportunity and obligation to live out every day in your marriage.

26. *Be angry and do not sin; do not let the sun go down on your anger,*
27. *and give no opportunity to the devil.*
    Avoid laying out a welcome mat for the enemy.
    Don't allow long-term unforgiveness or long periods of awkwardness.
29. *Let no corrupting talk come out of your mouths, but only such as is good for building up, as fits the occasion, that it may give grace to those who hear.*
30. *And do not grieve the Holy Spirit of God, by whom you were sealed for the day of redemption.*
31. *Let all bitterness and wrath and anger and clamor and slander be put away from you, along with all malice.*
    If you are born again, the Holy Spirit is working in you to conform you into the image of God. Allow the Spirit to do his work of redeeming you from anger and bitterness.
    Don't grieve the Spirit by giving in to anger or in saying corrupting words to your spouse in moments

*of frustration. Put away
an attitude of anger by
confessing it whenever it
surfaces and then turning
away from in in the power
of the Spirit.*

32 *Be kind to one another,
tenderhearted, forgiving one
another, as God in Christ
forgave you (Eph 4:26-27,
29-32).*

How you see your wife when she upsets you — and how you in turn respond — has everything to do with how you understand the way God sees you.

Jesus once told a parable about a servant who owed a significant amount of money to the king. When he was ordered to be sold along with his wife and children in order to pay the debt, the man fell on his knees and begged for mercy. Out of mercy, the king forgave the man his debt and released him. When that servant found someone who

owed him only a small amount, however, he grabbed the man, began choking him, and demanded, "pay what you owe me." When the man begged for mercy, the servant refused and had the man thrown in debtors prison.

The other servants were distressed when they saw this and reported it to the king. Jesus continues:

> *Then his master
> summoned him and
> said to him, 'You wicked
> servant! I forgave you all
> that debt because you
> pleaded with me. And
> should not you have had
> mercy on your fellow
> servant, as I had mercy
> on you?' And in anger his
> master delivered him to
> the jailers, until he should
> pay all his debt. So also my
> heavenly Father will do to
> every one of you, if you do
> not forgive your brother
> from your heart.
> (Matt 18:32-35)*

When we are born again, we have a great debt of grace. We are forgiven a debt we could never repay. We are like the wicked servant if we don't forgive our wives as generously as God forgave us.

In light of your debt to grace, lead in the race to repentance and forgiveness. ∞

> "We are like the wicked servant if we don't forgive our wives as generously as God forgave us."

Your Wife is Not One of the Boys

Peter tells men to show honor to their wives as the weaker vessel (1 Pet 3:7). What's he saying? What he's not saying is that your wife is of lesser value — because he clearly says to show her honor. She isn't of lesser value and she isn't morally or spiritually weaker than you. What we believe Peter has in mind here is just sheer physical weakness compared to the strength of a man.

So, how do you honor her as a weaker vessel? Well, you don't take advantage of your strength. You treat her with care. You don't lay hands on her to hurt her. You might be stronger than her physically, but Peter says treat her with honor.

In my (Randy's) house, we have two kinds of plates. We have some very durable plastic plates that the kids eat on. They cost 20 cents at Wal-mart and I don't care what you do to them. You can stomp on them, you can throw them across the kitchen, you can use them as a frisbee in the yard. It doesn't matter to me. If we lose or break one, we just throw it away and get another one.

We have some other plates in our house that if the kids even look at them, they're in trouble. Those plates are from great grandmothers and they're fragile. They're not as durable. They're weak and we treat them with care. We don't put them in the dishwasher. It's a rare and major event when we eat on them. And it's not because they're of lesser value, it's because they're of greater value. We treat these plates with more care, not less. We honor their value by treating them with special care and not being negligent.

Too many men treat their wives as one of the boys — durable and able to handle a lot of wear and tear. But your wife is not one of the boys. You honor her by treating her as a weaker vessel — by not taking advantage of your greater physical strength, but giving her special care and attention.

Lay your life down for your wife

Regardless of any examples or influences you may see around you of marriages that seek to be 50/50 and fully equal, it's your responsibility to lead and give 100 percent. Based on Ephesians 5:24, you're the head of your marriage as Christ is the head of the church. You are responsible to lead. You carry the burden when decisions need to be made and God will hold you accountable to lead.

And regardless of any examples or influences you may see around you of men who are dominating in their marriages, you are responsible to be a servant leader. Based on Ephesians 5:25, you are to love your wife "as Christ loved the church and gave himself up for her." In other words, you lovingly lead by laying down your life.

Just as we saw in the story of Jesus washing the disciples' feet in John 13, Christian leadership is sacrificial. Your leadership as a husband is modeled on the example of Christ who demonstrated his love as head of the church by laying down his life. That means your love and your leadership are not based on your emotions or on how your wife treats you, and they aren't tied up in any kind of score - keeping in which you only give based on what you get in return.

Instead, you anchor your love and leadership in Christ.

When you come home from work exhausted and just want to crash in front of the TV, you lay your life down to engage with your wife in a meaningful way. When you're eager to get back into a book you've been reading but see that your wife is troubled, you lay your life down to stop and help her process whatever is weighing her down.

When your wife is sick, you lay your life down to adjust your plans, give her the care she needs and pick up any house and family responsibilities she's not able to cover.

This is the kind of sacrifice that lovingly serves your wife, but also brings glory to God as it steadily chips away at your self-centeredness and remakes you into his image.

Live in an understanding way with your wife

A primary way that you lead in your marriage is in becoming an active student of her. "[H]usbands, live with your wives in an understanding way," the apostle Peter writes, "showing honor to the woman as the weaker vessel, since they are heirs with you of the grace of life, so that your prayers may not be hindered" (1 Pet 3:7).

Living with your wife in an understanding way means you're supposed to know her. You're not supposed to treat her generically — you're supposed to treat her uniquely. And in order to treat her uniquely, you have to work at knowing her.

People who know me [Randy], know that I'm not real keen on vegetables. Let's just suppose my wife wants to honor me this evening for a hard-working day and she says, "Honey, I love you so much and I want to honor you and so I've made you the best vegetable souffle I could make." Well, now I'm conflicted. She's shown an act of appreciation and kindness, but the way to my heart is through beef. And what I want to say is, "I'm grateful for this, but you don't even know me."

Some of your wives are saying, "You don't even know me — you're treating me generically." You can't do that. You have to treat your wife uniquely. So, how can you live with your wife in an understanding way? Study her, make intentional efforts based on what you learn, examine your marriage regularly, and lead in planning dates and getaways in order to provide the means in which most of these things can happen in a natural and enjoyable setting. And here's what all that looks like day to day:

Study her

You can't just read a book to find out how to live with your wife in an understanding way, you have to read your wife. Does she like walks more than flowers, flowers more than candy? You have to study her and learn about the unique person God has joined you to. You should seek to know answers to questions like these:

1. What blesses her?
2. What energizes her?
3. What five things is she good at?
4. What three ways has she shaped you for the better (for which you can thank her)?
5. Where does she think she's inadequate?
6. What's weighing on her heart today?

Make intentional efforts based on what you learn

Living in an understanding way means not only discerning what your wife needs and what blesses her but then acting on it. That means going into your week committed to do something with the answers to the previous questions and being discerning about opportunities that come your way.

1. Where can I weave into this week something that will bless my wife? (One way to stay on top of this is to keep building a list of things you know bless your wife, hints she drops and even a list of her sizes in your wallet or on your mobile device and to check that list regularly.)

2. How can I bring her encouragement in the areas she feels inadequate?

3. Where can I carve out time to pray about the things on my wife's heart today?

Examine your marriage regularly

How is your marriage doing? Where are you strong and where do you still need to grow? An important aspect of living with your wife in an understanding way is routinely setting aside time to review your marriage at a big-picture level. Some couples do a quick version of this once a week or as part of their date night once a month. This is a great time for you as a husband to ask, "What's something I can work on over the next 30 days?" — and to then review at your next check up. What can really pay off in this area is to do an annual or quarterly retreat where you can get away, have fun together and then spend time reviewing questions along the lines of the following:

1. What are the strengths and weaknesses of our home?

2. What are three ways we're being sanctified by our marriage (for example, I pray more, I take better care of my body, I listen better because you're in my life)?

3. What priceless things do we enjoy doing together that we need to protect on our calendar?

4. What one thing would we most like to see improve in the next 30 days, 90 days or year (based on when you plan to do a similar retreat)?

Lead in dating your wife

Few goals are achieved if they don't make it into your routine and few goals that do find a place in your routine fail to bear fruit. There is great power in turning resolutions into habits. The easiest way to consistently study your wife and examine your marriage is to lead in routinely dating your wife. Don't just wait until you're motivated to go out and definitely don't wait until there's no room in your schedule left for a date. Go ahead and block out a regular time and then lead in making the most out of your dates. Here's what that looks like:

1.

Take responsibility

Life will work against you. You can't wait for dates just to happen. Work, kids, and everything else will make demands on you. Your wife might have great recommendations and she might initiate some special dates, but you should take on the primary responsibility for making sure that you have a regular date together.

2.

Plan

Make sure it happens. Arrange the babysitter. Come up with the plan. This takes leadership, but it demonstrates that you are thinking of your wife and providing for her. You might think it shows deference to tell your wife, "Oh, I don't care where we go tonight, you decide," but it actually shows a lack of leadership and investment. Be willing to be flexible on your plans in case she's not crazy about your idea, but lead with an offer.

Focus on connection

Your dates don't have to be elaborate. Your wife would rather have a bean burrito and your undivided attention than a rib-eye. But make sure your date accommodates good conversation time. If you take your wife to a movie, add dinner because you can't (or shouldn't be) having a long conversation during a movie.

Work around challenges

A tight budget, a new baby, bad weather, or some other kind of challenge shouldn't keep you from dating your wife. In fact, it's even more important to keep dating and connecting when a baby is born, when money is tight or something else is posing a challenge in your marriage. Working around these kinds of challenges will just require a little more creativity. Try having a special at-home date after the kids go down — move your table by the fireplace, light some candles and turn on some music and you can rival the romance of lots of expensive restaurants in your wife's eyes. Or just go take a walk. Walks are not only free, they provide fresh air — something that's especially valuable if your wife has been indoors most of the day.

Explore some fresh options

If your dates have gotten into a rut, explore some new options. Ask friends for suggestions, do a Web search for local favorites and make a list to keep handy. Consider these options: do a progressive date night (with appetizers at one restaurant, dinner at another and dessert at a third place), go to a shooting range, try food from a different nationality (if you typically have Chinese, Italian, or Indian, try Cuban, German, Thai, or Vietnamese), take flowers as a couple to a widow from your church, or play ping-pong. Just think fresh and creatively.

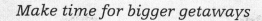

6. ## Make time for bigger getaways

Each quarter or at least once a year, plan for a longer getaway where you can make a bigger investment in your marriage. You don't have to break the bank or cash in on all your vacation days for this, but it is worth arranging for at least an overnight stay and even for a little travel time to add anticipation and extra time for conversation. Make the getaway as stress-free as possible for your wife by taking the lead on all the arrangements, including child and pet care.

7. ## Plan surprises

Any date or getaway can be more special when you make it a surprise. Sure, there's always risk in planning something that might have a scheduling conflict or that your wife might not like as much as you had hoped, but there's great reward in being the fun captain who can navigate all the logistics and successfully pull off a surprise.

WARNING: When it comes to leading, many men talk a better game than they play. Whether it's in your work, your marriage, your family, or your local church, you can't just tell people what you intend to do.
In your marriage, don't go home and say, "Honey, things are going to be different around here. Here are five things I'm gonna start doing." Just lead. Don't announce it. At the first opportunity you get, just do it. Let her discover it. The last thing you want to do is over-promise and under-deliver.

- Dan Dumas

Lead in faithful intimacy

When you are one with your wife — physically, emotionally, and spiritually — you bear the image of God. Your oneness reflects the sacrificial love of Christ and His church (Eph 5:22-32) as well as the oneness and fellowship between the Father and the Son (John 17:20-23).

This connection is made even more obvious in Paul's letter to the Corinthians where he explains how sexual sin distinctly wars against God's design for oneness in the body of faith and in marriage:

Do you not know that your bodies are members of Christ? Shall I then take the members of Christ and make them members of a prostitute? Never! Or do you not know that he who is joined to a prostitute becomes one body with her? For, as it is written, "The two will become one flesh." But he who is joined to the Lord becomes one spirit with him. Flee from sexual immorality. Every other sin a person commits is outside the body, but the sexually immoral person sins against his own body. Or do you not know that your body is a temple of the Holy Spirit within you, whom you have from God? You are not your own, for you were bought with a price. So glorify God in your body. (1 Cor 6:15-20)

Satan is not unaware of this truth. As he prowls around seeking to devour (1 Pet 5:8), he knows he can distort the truth of God's oneness and love to a watching world by attacking the oneness in your marriage. This is ground zero. Your leadership is essential at this point in order to ensure the area that can bring the deepest joy and pleasure in your marriage doesn't become the source of Satan's greatest victory against you, your wife, and God's reflection in your marriage.

Your leadership is crucial in three specific areas: sanctification, redeemed desire, and prioritization.

SANCTIFICATION

"For this is the will of God," Paul writes to the Thessalonians, "your sanctification." Sanctification is the essential work that begins after Jesus justifies you before the Father and presents you blameless. It's the process of growing to be holy as God is holy. In the same breath where Paul says that God's will is your sanctification, he immediately adds, "that you abstain from sexual immorality; that each one of you know how to control his own body in holiness and honor, not in the passion of lust like the Gentiles who do not know God;" (1 Thess 4:3-6).

The Spirit is at work to guide your sanctification, but you have to be active in this work as well — especially in abstaining from sexual immorality and in controlling your body. This is where you work with the empowerment of the Spirit to develop self-mastery over the flesh. It involves being watchful, putting distance between yourself and sin, and rushing to repent when you do sin.

• **Be watchful:** In our sex-saturated culture, you have to be alert to temptations that can hit you everywhere you turn and can begin to pull you away from oneness with your wife. You have to lead in being watchful (1 Cor 16:13; 1 Peter 5:8) of your surroundings and in being on guard where you know you're most likely to be tempted.

• **Put distance between yourself and sin:** "[M]ake no provision for the flesh, to gratify its desires," Paul writes to the Romans. "Abstain from sexual immorality" he writes to the Thessalonians (1 Thess 4:3b). "But sexual immorality and all impurity or covetousness must not even be named among you," he writes to the Ephesians (Eph 5:3). "Flee sexual immorality," (1 Cor 6:18) he writes to the Corinthians. "Put to death therefore what is earthly in you: sexual immorality, impurity, passion, evil desire" he writes to the Colossians (Col 3:5a). Paul's choice of words — abstain, make no provision, flee, put to death, and so forth — makes it clear that you should actively distance yourself from sexual immorality. That means guarding your eyes, words, and thought life from any images, conversations, or wandering thoughts that could be a gateway to sexual immorality.

• **Be repentant:** As born-again men, we are still prone to sin. "If we say we have no sin, we deceive ourselves, and the truth is not in us," the apostle John writes, but then he adds, "If we confess our sins, he is faithful and just to forgive us our sins and to cleanse us from all unrighteousness" (1 John 1:8-9). James writes, "sin when it is fully grown brings forth death" (Jas 1:15). Don't be surprised by the reality of sin in your life as a believer, but don't let unrepentant sin grow toward death.

REDEEMED DESIRE

While it's true that sexual temptation will be with you throughout your life, it is possible to significantly change how you fight temptation by allowing the Spirit to redeem your driving desires.

Desire is a powerful engine when it comes to intimacy in your marriage. The most effective way to fight sexual temptation is to let God do an engine replacement — to change out the engine of fleshly desire that drives you toward sin and death with a Spirit-driven engine that drives you toward abundant life. Paul shows what that looks like in his letter to the Galatians:

But I say, walk by the Spirit, and you will not gratify the desires of the flesh. For the desires of the flesh are against the Spirit, and the desires of the Spirit are against the flesh, for these are opposed to each other, to keep you from doing the things you want to do. But if you are led by the Spirit, you are not under the law. Now the works of the flesh are evident: sexual immorality, impurity, sensuality, idolatry, sorcery, enmity, strife, jealousy, fits of anger, rivalries, dissensions, divisions, envy, drunkenness, orgies, and things like these. I warn you, as I warned you before, that those who do such things will not inherit the kingdom of God. But the fruit of the Spirit is love, joy, peace, patience, kindness, goodness, faithfulness, gentleness, self-control; against such things there is no law. And those who belong to Christ Jesus have crucified the flesh with its passions and desires. (Gal 5:16-24)

As you crucify the desires of the flesh, you won't have to keep struggling to throttle the desires that lead to sin and death (Jas 1:14-15). Instead, you can submit to the Spirit and allow the desires of the Spirit to drive you toward

> **"Give your kids the security of knowing that your marriage is secure and thriving by preserving dedicated time with your wife."**

deeper intimacy and oneness with your wife.

As the Spirit leads you and produces fruit in your life and your marriage, remember the wisdom of Solomon to continually cultivate your desire for your wife:

> *Drink water from your own cistern, flowing water from your own well.*
> *Should your springs be scattered abroad, streams of water in the streets?*
> *Let them be for yourself alone, and not for strangers with you.*
> *Let your fountain be blessed, and rejoice in the wife of your youth, a lovely deer, a graceful doe.*
> *Let her breasts fill you at all times with delight; be*

intoxicated always in her love. (Prov 5:15-19)

Enjoy the wife God has given you as a good gift to be received with thanksgiving (1 Tim 4:1-5). Celebrate your love together. Drink deeply of her love.

PRIORITIZATION

Finally, lead in prioritizing oneness with your wife. As you faithfully lead in your work, your responsibilities as a father, and your commitments in the local church, remember that oneness with your wife is a source of stability to keep you grounded and replenished for all of your responsibilities. She is your helper for the work God has given you to do.

So, prioritize oneness with her. Hold all your responsibilities in tension with your responsibilities to her. Give her the first hug and kiss when you walk in the door from work — even as your kids race to you with updates about their day. Give your kids the security of knowing your marriage is secure and thriving by preserving dedicated time with your wife (that goes for regular date nights as well as regular times at night of uninterrupted time for you and your wife to catch up). This is what it takes to regularly grow in oneness and intimacy — just make it a priority. ⊠

Lead your wife spiritually

A significant, but often under-emphasized area where you are called to lead in your marriage is as a spiritual leader. You are to disciple your wife and serve in her sanctification. This is true of all believers according to Hebrews 10:24 that says, "let us consider how to stir up one another to love and good works," but it's especially true of husbands who bear the responsibility to lead in a marriage. Your marriage should be a significant source of your wife's sanctification. Consider Paul's words to the Ephesians again:

Husbands, love your wives, as Christ loved the church and gave himself up for her, that he might sanctify her, having cleansed her by the washing of water with the word, so that he might present the church to himself in splendor, without spot or wrinkle or any such thing, that she might be holy and without blemish. In the same way husbands should love their wives as their own bodies.

He who loves his wife loves himself. (Eph 5:25-28)

Clearly, you're not Christ. There is a sanctifying work that only Jesus can do, but as you model your love on the sanctifying relationship of Christ in the church, you do have a role in your wife's sanctification. Even if your wife is more spiritually engaged and mature than you are, you still have a responsibility to lead. Your leadership is not directly tied to your biblical knowledge or spiritual engagement, but to the fact that God has given you responsibility as the head of your marriage (Eph 5:23-24). If you are not doing anything to lead in this area, you need a plan and a trajectory toward leading.

That starts with growing in your own sanctification. Seek the face of God each day before seeing the face of man. Rise early and call out to God for your own growth and then for wisdom in how to serve your wife in her growth. It's important to stay focused on your personal sanctification as a reminder that even though you're the leader, you aren't the standard for spiritual

What does your marriage say about the gospel?

Your marriage is supposed to say something and it's supposed to say something about the gospel according to Ephesians 5:22-33. Actually, your marriage is already saying something about the gospel. But is what it's saying true? Is it accurate? The furthering of the gospel is at stake here.

People are watching your marriage. In fact, they can tell a lot from the countenance of your wife's face. Do they see the joy of a wife who is flourishing because her husband is leading well and caring deeply for her? If you treat your wife harshly, if you don't live with her in an understanding way, or if you don't honor her, then you are saying something that's not true about the gospel.

God give us the courage and resolve to lead well — to accurately portray the gospel in our marriages — not just so that our prayers may not be hindered, but so that the gospel would not be hindered and that Jesus Christ would be exalted.

---

maturity — you are called to help your wife conform to God, not to you.

So how can you lead your wife spiritually? You don't have to set up a pulpit in your bedroom or schedule intensive discipleship classes before bedtime. Instead, make it a natural part of your life together:

- Show leadership in getting your family actively engaged in your local church.
- Recommend books that you can read and discuss with your wife.
- Lead in finding conferences to attend, messages to watch online, and other means to grow in the Word together and to spur each other on in the faith.
- If you have children, take the lead in creating opportunities to worship together as a family in your home. This can be as simple as extended family dinner time to include Bible reading and prayer or can be expanded to be a mini-church service in your home.
- Finally, pray with your wife. It's tragic how many husbands never do. The simplest and most regular way to lead your wife spiritually is to pray with her every day — to help her bring her burdens to the Lord through your intercession on her behalf. ∞

A
—
GUIDE
—
FOR
—
FATHERS

Deuteronomy 6:4-8

Hear, O Israel: The LORD our God, the LORD is one. You shall love the LORD your God with all your heart and with all your soul and with all your might. And these words that I command you today shall be on your heart. You shall teach them diligently to your children, and shall talk of them when you sit in your house, and when you walk by the way, and when you lie down, and when you rise. You shall bind them as a sign on your hand, and they shall be as frontlets between your eyes. You shall write them on the doorposts of your house and on your gates.

Proverbs 1:8-9

Hear, my son, your father's instruction, and forsake not your mother's teaching, for they are a graceful garland for your head and pendants for your neck.

Colossians 3:21

Fathers, do not provoke your children, lest they become discouraged.

Ephesians 6:4

Fathers, do not provoke your children to anger, but bring them up in the discipline and instruction of the Lord.

Engaged leadership at home

"Engage Bob!" That's the plea Helen Parr resorted to in the 2004 movie "The Incredibles" as her husband, the former superhero Mr. Incredible, slowly descended into anything but incredible in his role as father.

Biblical manhood faces some of it's greatest challenges where it's most needed: in the home. The relationship between fathers and their children is too often minimalistic and punctuated by anger and volatility. Men who are able to lead well in the marketplace or even in the local church too often find their homes unmanagable and resort to survival or escape tactics as their default form of fathering. These dads typically protect their families from harm and

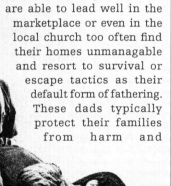

provide the resources their children need in order to be sheltered, clothed, fed, educated, and entertained but find it frustrating to provide much else.

But all the leadership traits we've considered so far apply to your responsibilities as a father — this is prime time. Fatherhood requires engaged leadership, but it's all about serving others. As a result, you have to transition from any role you might have at work where you lead others into a context of service at home. You go home to serve and give yourself a way. Your leadership isn't toward yourself — it's always directed toward others.

Home is the place where your leadership will be needed around the clock and where your vulnerabilities will be most obvious, but it's also the place where you have the potential to bear the most fruit as you shape little hearts for eternity.

So what does leadership look like for a father and how can you be intentional in shaping your children for heaven? Based on the ground we've covered so far and a basic framework of Scriptures (including Eph 6, Deut 6:4-9, Col 3:20-21 and Prov 1-9), the material that follows represents what we believe to be biblically faithful wisdom for you as a father.

Nine areas to lead with intention

How is a man, particularly in his home, supposed to express his masculinity as the leader? As a suggestion, here are nine areas where a man should initiate in the home:

1.

Vision: This is where we are going

The leader in the home is the primary keeper of the vision. Like John F. Kennedy and his moon shot, you take responsibility for having a bold vision for the next decade or so. It's your job to ask, "what do we want this family to look like 10-15 years from now?" You can develop the vision in consensus with your wife (and children if they are of the age to give meaningful input) but you need to initiate it. This is the big picture of what priorities your family should have, what you want your family to look like (we want our sons to be biblically masculine and our daughters to be biblically feminine, we want to be active members of our local church, etc.), what kind of home environment you want (honoring to God, family members encouraging one another, no rivalries, etc.). If you don't set the vision, who will?

2.

Direction: This is how we get there

Here is where you map out the details of the vision. These are the daily, weekly, and monthly steps you are going to take in order to bring about the vision you have already agreed on. For instance, you plan to take your wife on a weekly date night and to take your children out individually two times per month, each. You plan to go camping four times per year. You get the point. Additionally, this means going into each week with purpose — asking on Sunday, "What should I do in each of my roles to fulfill our family vision this week?" "Is there a conversation I need to have this week?" "Is there an event I should take advantage of?" If you have a good vision, but no direction, it's not going to work. You may want your sons to learn how to play baseball (vision) but if you never throw a ball with them (direction) they will not learn. You do not need to produce a 50-page document but you do need to land on some basic steps to bring your vision to life.

3. Instruction: Let me show you how

Plugging things into your routine such as date nights with your kids, camping and baseball practice can take you a long way, but much of what you need to pass along to your kids requires your specific instruction. There are dozens of times each week when "Go ask you mother" is not going to be an adequate response to the inquiries of your children, if you want to be a good leader in your home. Each time your kids asks questions you have an opportunity to give instruction. But you should also be proactive. On a regular basis, find a way to rehearse possible scenarios with your children: What happens if someone says [fill in the blank] to you? What will you do? What happens if someone is bothering your sister? It's inspiring for your children to get this kind of authoritative instruction from their dad. It shows that you're not asking them to go it alone, but you're going to show them exactly what to do.

4. Imitation: Watch me

This is the heart of leadership isn't it? There is no room for, "Do what I say and not what I do." That is failed leadership. What you want to give are inspiring examples and clear demonstrations of proper living before God. For instance, you should tell your children, "If I say it, you can say it. If I don't say it, you don't say it." This will give you remarkable consciousness of your own speech, and it will inspire your children that proper speech can be achieved. What happens if you say the wrong words? Then you demonstrate something else for your children: the apology. "I am sorry I said that, it was not appropriate, will you forgive me?" Many men think they should never apologize to their children for moments of sin and failure (for fear it demonstrates weakness), but this only hardens the heart of a child (and a wife for that matter) toward their father (or husband). A good leader says with the Apostle Paul, "follow me inasmuch as I follow Christ." This means making restitution for the times when you sin and fail. Hardly anything can be more powerful in the life of your family.

Inspiration: Isn't this great?

As the leader in the home, you are responsible for the morale of the group. You must regularly instill in the members of your family that this is one great clan. Who else, outside of your home, is going to do this? Let's face it, there is not a constant state of euphoria in any home, but there should be a constant reminder from the leader that he thinks this thing is great. This is something you can say as you're heading out for work in the morning, when you get home from work, when you're putting your kids to bed at night, or at special moments along the way. You can say it however you want, but find a way to say something like, "This is an awesome family." Of course, your family isn't perfect. They are going to do things that frustrate you, but they need you to find the grace to encourage them where you can. Additionally, your family needs you to leave your stress at the office. You can have a challenging day, but you shouldn't drag your family down as a result. You don't have the luxury of moping. You need to keep the morale up.

Affirmation: You're doing great

Everyone needs affirmation and they need it from the one who is leading them. The greatest leaders in the world are those who know how to encourage and inspire. The leader is responsible for overall morale and the key to this is individual encouragement. You must regularly pull your children aside and say, "I'm proud of you, you're doing great, I'm thrilled to be your dad, etc." This is doubly important for your wife. You're going to be in big trouble if someone else is encouraging your wife more than you are. In a culture that is constantly pushing children away from their fathers and wives away from their husbands, the impact of affirmation is amazing and powerful.

Evaluation: How are we doing?

This is the hardest one. Men do not like to self-evaluate because we tend to think much more highly of ourselves than we ought.

But the leader must regularly stick his head up, look around, and see if this thing is going where it should. This is one of the true burdens of leadership and you must bear it. Sometimes it is the recognition that your schedule has gotten a little out of control and you have to restructure your time. Sometimes you realize that you spoke harshly to your wife or one of your children and you need to clear the air. Evaluation is something you have to do regularly.

8.

Correction: Let's make a change

In his epistle, James writes "Anyone who listens to the word but does not do what it says is like someone who looks at his face in a mirror and, after looking at himself, goes away and immediately forgets what he looks like" (Jas 1:23-24). In the same way, evaluation is no good unless you agree on a plan to make the needed corrections. But again, you must initiate this process. It is a necessary part of good leadership. Findings from your evaluation need to lead to changes in your priorities, your calendar, etc.

9.

Protection and provision: I'll take care of you

The overarching message of men leading in the home is "I'll take care of you." This sentiment is expressed with great humility and with the full knowledge that no man can protect his family from every possible harm. It is done with the intention of communicating, "I will never leave you, I will spend my last drop of energy and love and life taking care of you, and I can be counted on by God's grace." Fathers die, husbands lose their jobs and have no work, and tragedy comes into the lives of children (like cancer and other illnesses) that no father can protect against. But there is still some sense in which a man should communicate this general principle to his wife and children. Even in these tragedies and difficulties, you can exercise your protection and provision by modeling your own dependence upon the Lord and in doing so, you can protect your home from bitterness and ill feelings toward the Lord. It's in this way that you show your protection and provision until the end of this life and build anticipation for the life to come.

Raising future
men and women

When our grandparents were raising our parents, popular culture was not as dramatically at odds with the biblical understandings of gender as it is now. The current cultural confusion over gender, however, requires parents to be highly intentional if they want to raise masculine sons and feminine daughters.

There are no generic people. There are men, and there are women. Consequently there are no generic Christian people. There are Christian men and there are Christian women. In Genesis 1-2, Ephesians 5, 1 Peter 3, and Colossians 3, we find clarity about the primary roles of men and women. There are differing ways in which men and women will live out the Christian life. For instance, when giving specific instruction and admonition to men, the Bible usually does so within three key categories: leading, providing, and protecting. In other words, biblical masculinity involves a heart that is inclined to obey God within this particular context of leadership, provision and protection. This may take place predominantly as husbands and fathers, but it still should be cultivated, encouraged and instilled in boys as they mature into manhood.

To that end, Christian parents should cultivate, teach and encourage the distinct characteristics of biblical manhood and womanhood. Both mom and dad share this task, but fathers bear the responsibility to lead it, to model manhood and to make distinctive contributions in their sons and daughters.

Here are the ways you should be actively involved:

GIVE VISION

Give your children a clear vision for biblical masculinity and femininity. There is certainly some subjectivity here, but you and your wife should agree on the behaviors and inclinations necessary to carry out the roles assigned to men and women and then decide how those can be cultivated in your sons and/or daughters. Since the Bible teaches that the role of wife, mother, and keeper of the home

> "Christian parents should cultivate, teach, and encourage the distinct characteristics of biblical manhood and womanhood."

is a high calling for women, then you and your wife should instill and cultivate the desire and skill to embrace this high call — with your wife naturally having a more highlighted role. Since the Bible teaches that men are to be leaders, providers, and protectors, then you and your wife should instill and cultivate the desire and skill to undertake these responsibilities — with you taking the lead.

MODEL IT

Next, you and your wife have to model what you want to cultivate. Husbands and wives living out their proper roles together not only impact the marriage but also impact how children understand their own gender identity. Since role relationships are inherent in the created order, it naturally causes a certain amount of dissonance for children who are watching parents live contrary to their roles.

This is especially significant for boys. When they are born, boys and girls develop a natural bond with their mom as she feeds and nurtures them. A girl becoming a woman can just stay close to her mom. A boy, however, has to reach the place where he says, "I'm not this — I'm different from mom" and then he has to move toward dad and say, "I'm this." This is disruptive. It's not a sign of disrespect or a rejection of femininity. It's just a transition that has to happen for boys to grow into men.

If mom clings to the boy too much or there's not a man to gravitate toward, a boy may overwhelmingly identity with his mom and act like her or he might know in his gut that he's equipped for something else and end up reacting in conflict and resentment that he can't articulate. A dad who leads, provides, and protects gives a boy a model to identify with. A strong dad can also discourage a boy from disrespecting his mom in the transition — and instead teach him to honor her as a woman as he follows a path to manhood. This is key for teaching your son how to treat his future wife.

> "You should intentionally create moments of risk, valor, and adventure (even if they are only perceived as such)."

Ultimately, you need to model manhood and then be able to answer your son's (often unspoken) question: "Am I becoming a man?"

TEACH AUTHORITY

You have to teach your son to learn to submit to authority. Because one day he's going to have it and he won't be able to wield it correctly if he hasn't learned how to show it to others first.

You also have to help your daughter to recognize good authority. Some day, a man is going to be responsible for sacrificially leading your daughter as a wife. It's your job to make the transition into a future marriage as smooth as possible. When you give your daughter's hand in marriage to her groom's hand on her wedding day, you want it to be a strong hand-off.

AFFIRM MANHOOD AND WOMANHOOD

Children are not generic and neither is their behavior. Affirm your sons in their masculinity and your daughters in their femininity. Let them know you are glad God made them the way he did. When your daughters exhibit characteristics that will make them effective moms or wives, say, "you're going to be a great mom." When you observe particularly masculine behavior, say, "that's good leadership," or "that's what men do." Boys inherently want to be like their dads and girls want to be like their moms. They need to be encouraged in their progress with gender-specific language.

Affirm manhood and womanhood in your affection for your children as well. Wrestle with your boys, give them slaps on the back, high-fives, bear hugs, shoulder punches, and other forms of physical engagement as a regular connection. It's important to consistently show affection to your daughters as well. They might enjoy horseplay with you as well, but be intentional to also honor their femininity. Hold their hands. Kiss their cheeks. Give them hugs. This kind of affection can be challenging when your daughter starts changing into a young woman, but that's when she'll need it most. A good way to develop

If you want your sons to be resilient and inclined to lead, you should create moments for training through sports, and other structured activities that involve challenge, l e a d e r s h i p opportunities, and discipline. In addition to those settings, you should intentionally create moments of risk, valor, and adventure (even if they are only perceived as such).

For example, if you're camping or hiking a trail you can build instincts in your sons by asking what they would do if they encountered a bear and then practicing scenarios. When you encounter challenges like someone dropping gear down a slope off the path you can give your boys an opportunity to be a hero. "Uh-oh, mom dropped her lantern down that steep ridge. I don't know how steady that ground is there or what kind of threatening insects or vegetation are over there off the trail, but I need you boys to take care of it." Let them believe it's all riding on them. Perception is reality. Build courage in your boys. Incline their hearts and cultivate their instincts toward resilience and toughness. ⊠

and continue a habit of affirming your daughter and showing her appropriate affection is to have a regular daddy-daughter date. With a set time to give each other your complete attention, you can draw her out and support her path to womanhood.

CREATE MOMENTS OF TRAINING

Finally, be intentional in providing distinctive opportunities for training. If you want your children to be proficient at the piano, you'll provide lessons. Similarly, if you want your daughters to be inclined to motherhood and homemaking, then (with your wife having a more highlighted role) you'll involve your daughters in activities and training that prepare them to manage a home and care for a family.

Twenty-five things a dad should teach a boy

Before the industrial revolution, it was common for men to spend much of their day in the company of their sons — either on the family farm or in the family business. In those settings, dads could teach their sons practical lessons as well as the lessons of leadership, protection, and provision expected of manhood.

Today, work, school, extracurricular activities, and even church take fathers and sons in separate directions. Dads, therefore, have to be intentional about creating the opportunities to teach their sons — to model manhood, to teach industry and resourcefulness. One way to do that is to work through a list of things that fathers can teach sons. You can work through such a list in one of two ways: either 1) by setting aside a regular father/son time to take on one item at a time (one dad started this routine and calls it "Manhood Mondays") or by 2) just taking the time to instruct your son anytime you're about to do one of these tasks yourself, It's not efficient, but the investment of your time can be priceless. Whether you do it proactively, reactively or both, what matters most is taking the time to build a legacy with your son(s).

Don't freak out by what is or isn't on the list here. These are meant to be examples of what engagement looks like, but you can adapt this or just see it as a head-start for your own list. You'll notice that many of the skills listed here can be bypassed by modern technology in most industrially advance countries. Making the effort to teach these, however, will give you valuable time with your son(s) and will give you a practical opportunity to present principles of leading, protecting and providing, all the while building confidence in their abilities as emerging men.

1. Speak in public — there's power in the spoken word.
2. Read good books — leaders are readers.
3. Play an instrument — especially because of the discipline required.
4. Play individual, two-person and team sports.
5. Build a fire.
6. Camp out — pitch the tent, cook stuff over the fire, the whole thing.
7. Carve a turkey.
8. Light a grill.
9. Jump start a car.
10. Tie a knot — such as a bowline, square knot, taut-line, and figure eight among others.
11. Use basic tools — hammer, saw, wrench, screwdriver.
12. Paint a room — trim and all.
13. Handle a gun and a knife — for safety, protection, sport, and hunting.
14. Skin an animal.
15. Be a gentleman — open doors, stand when a woman approaches at dinner, etc.
16. Grow stuff — and not just a Chia pet.
17. Iron a shirt — and do laundry and other work around the house in a manly way.
18. Manage money — keep a balanced checkbook, show generosity, and learn basic saving and investing.
19. Shake a hand — strong shake (save the tuna for dinner) and look 'em in the eye.
20. Give a man hug — skip the side hug, and go arms spread eagle with bold back slaps.
21. Keep vows.
22. Dress like a gentleman — coordinate pants, shirts, jackets, ties, belts, socks, etc. appropriately to the occasion.
23. Tip — for example at least 15% for a waiter providing adequate service, $1 for a checked coat, $1 per bag for curbside check in at airport, etc.
24. Serve others — shovel walks, help with heavy loads, etc.
25. Handle loss — sports and games in preparation for loss in work and relationships.

Take me out to the ballgame: Baseball, biblical masculinity, and godly character

by Randy Stinson

Baseball, otherwise known in our home as the greatest sport ever played, is the sport of choice for our family. And it's something I've found to be a distinct tool for building Christian character and cultivating biblical masculinity.

WHY WE LOVE BASEBALL FOR CHARACTER BUILDING

We believe that sports in general can help us observe our children in various contexts to see how their character is developing. As a dad it is particularly important to me. I am gone during the day because of vocational responsibilities and since my job is such that I cannot bring my children with me (such as a farming situation) I do not have the opportunity to see them in a crisis or under pressure.

Baseball helps me with this. Since the game is played at a slower pace than some sports, each play, and player, is highlighted on every pitch. You do not need to watch the game film later to know who missed a fly ball, who struck out, or who got thrown out stealing second base. I can easily observe what my sons do when they miss a ground ball, when they strike out, and when they are put in to pitch under a pressure situation with no outs and bases loaded.

The game is so full of subjectivity that I can easily see them in situations when they are treated unfairly. A ball is called a strike. A safe slide into third is called out. And most of the time, because of the easy access to players in the dugout, I can make mid-game character corrections, without waiting until we all get home.

I can see what they do when they lose big and when they win big. It gives me an opportunity to see what comes out of them in situations that I cannot possibly manufacture at home. I am not living for the day when my sons become the next Derek Jeter or Alex Rodriguez. In fact, I would generally not wish the life of a professional baseball player on anyone. And although we love to play the game, we are not living for it. It is a parental tool that also happens to be really fun.

Eleven connecting points between baseball, biblical masculinity and godly character

———

1. **Play ball: Umpires and understanding authority**

   Once a player steps out onto the field, the umpires control the game. There are an enormous number of subjective calls. Entire games can hinge on any of these decisions. There is no instant replay (yet!), and baseball is notorious for its "colorful" interactions between coaches, fans, players, and umpires.

   What I want my sons to understand is that submitting to the judgment of the umpires is part of the game. Imperfect authorities are going to make mistakes, they are going to sometimes show favoritism and they are sometimes going to avenge a rude fan or disruptive coach.

   We trust in a sovereign God who is meticulous in overseeing all things and in our life will use unfair employers, rude people, poor judgment, and the like, to shape us into the image of Christ.

   PRINCIPLE FOR MANHOOD:

   You do not argue with the umpire. You do not express disgust or disappointment with the umpire. That is the coach's prerogative. You do not blame the outcome of the game on the umpire and you do not use him as an excuse because your team did not play well.

2. **Take one for the team: Self-sacrifice and toughness**

   "Take one for the team" is a common expression in baseball that usually means leaning in and getting hit by a pitch intentionally. On an inside pitch, the batter turns his hip in slightly allowing himself to be hit in the back area and thereby getting a free walk to first base. This type of sacrifice can many times be the difference-maker in a game, both in terms of score and morale.

   Yes, it hurts, hence "take one for the team." But every baseball player knows that self-sacrifice and toughness wins games. This may sound harsh, but every fan knows it is part of baseball, and every man knows it is crucial to

being masculine. Intentionally putting oneself in harm's way for the good of another is at the heart of masculinity and only one who has cultivated a sense of toughness will be willing to do it. This notion points us to Christ, who set his face like flint to Jerusalem and the cross, willingly bearing the Father's wrath for the sins of his people.

PRINCIPLE FOR MANHOOD: Get hit by the pitch if necessary or unavoidable. Then run to first base as if nothing happened. The men in the stands all high-five because they know there is a shortness of toughness, and they just saw some. Remember, "there is no crying in baseball!"

3. **Slide! Obedience to authority**

Coaches are central to the game of baseball. While umpires represent an ultimate authority, coaches are the generals on the field, making all sorts of key decisions that will impact the outcome of the game.

One of the hardest things for young boys to do is listen to their coach's base-running instructions. Often I see a young boy stop at first while his coach is yelling, "go to second!" because the boy "didn't think he could make it." Or I observe a young player running to second — trying be wise in his own eyes, he's watching the ball in the outfield instead of his third base coach. Games have been won or lost by good and bad base running. Coaches continually have to tell young players if the coach makes the call, he will take the blame.

Authority is given by God for our protection. We should listen to those who have charge over us. Home, church, government, and even the Godhead, all have a structure that involves authority. It is part of the stamp of God on all of creation.

PRINCIPLE FOR MANHOOD: Submit to the coach. Move in when he says to move in. Play

deep when he says to play deep. Bunt when he says bunt. Run when he says run and slide when he says slide.

4. **You're out! Unfairness** Because men are called to be leaders, providers, and protectors, they need to be accustomed to dealing with unfairness. The world is full of it.

One of the ways I determine maturity levels of my sons is how they respond to unfairness. Many times on the field they are direct recipients. On the pitcher's mound, the umpire calls a ball that was clearly a strike. At the plate, the umpire calls a strike that was clearly a ball. Playing shortstop, the umpire says you missed the tag you know you made.

How do they respond in those moments? Do they pout or throw their glove down? In certain cases, appeals may be made, but a man knows that in a fallen world, unfairness abounds, and God will sort these things out according to his pleasure.

PRINCIPLE FOR MANHOOD: You do not cry or stomp your feet. You do not throw your glove, bat, or helmet. Move on to the next play.

5. **Strike 3! Failure** The dreaded strike out. It is one of the worst feelings in baseball. You stepped up to the plate, had at least three opportunities and failed, and now you are walking back to the dugout with fans and peers looking on. Your failure is abundantly obvious.

Hitting a pitched ball is notoriously one of the most difficult tasks in all of sports. With a 30 percent success rate being deemed high, the odds are that you are going to fail.

PRINCIPLE FOR MANHOOD: You do not pout, hit the ground with the bat, throw your helmet, look incredulously at the umpire, or go to the dugout and sulk. Those responses are childish, hurt morale, and reveal a serious character flaw. You are going to fail. Baseball teaches it every inning. By its very nature, baseball is a humbling game.

6. **When you can't find the plate: Humility** Sometimes, even the most consistent pitchers have outings when they just cannot "find the plate." Usually possessing great control, a pitcher cannot, for some reason, throw a strike. Few things are worse than being the center of attention, unable to perform a duty that you know you can normally perform.

Recently, one of my sons found himself in this position. As ball after ball, walk and walk mounted up, it was obvious he just could not "find the plate." Most parents hate for their sons to be pulled from a game. Not me. I was relieved when the coach, on his own, ended the fiasco.

In the car, after the game, I led my son to pray a prayer of gratitude for the humiliation. Why? Because it was a gift. God opposes the proud and gives grace to the humble. The cultivation of humility in a poor pitching performance should cultivate gratitude to God.

PRINCIPLE FOR MANHOOD: Practice hard and play the game well, but see the bobbled ground balls, failure to find the plate, overthrows, and missed fly balls as evidence of God's mercy to you as he places things in your life to help you become humble. You do not want to live in such a way that you invite the active opposition of God.

7. **Keep a short memory: Resilience** One of the most important skills to cultivate in baseball is keeping

a short memory. A swing and a miss has to be immediately forgotten because another pitch is coming. A missed ground ball has to be immediately forgotten because another batter is coming to the plate. A dropped pop fly must be immediately forgotten because another one is surely on the way.

The phrase, "keep a short memory" encourages the cultivation of resilience. It is good for a young man to get knocked down, only to have to get right back up again. Biblical masculinity requires resilience, a godly toughness.

PRINCIPLE FOR MANHOOD: In the wake of a mistake or botched play, your personal disappointment must be secondary to the next play, which will be happening... approximately five seconds from now. Self-preoccupation and self-pity are enemies of masculinity.

8. **Winners and losers: Grace, mercy and honor** This is not the part about "its how you play the game." This is where it's time to remember that someone wins and someone loses. My concern for my sons is how they act in each situation.

When they are winning big, do they taunt the other team or laugh at their poor play? When they are losing big, do they pout, cry, or make excuses (the umpire, the weather)? While competition can be bad, I think there is something inherent in us that strives for victory and loathes defeat. Genesis 3:15 illustrates a profound struggle and a crushing victory. Paul uses language of competition when he alludes to contending for the gospel (Jude 3) and also striving for sanctification (1 Cor 9:24-27).

PRINCIPLE FOR MANHOOD: The inward desire to embrace victory and avoid defeat is an opportunity to point ourselves to the gospel. In our losses, we congratulate our opponent on their great victory and commit to strengthen our weaknesses. In our great victories, we honor our opponent by extending grace.

9. **Thanks coach: Gratitude** As with most youth sports, baseball is carried on the shoulders of thousands of volunteers. Each week my sons have opportunities to express gratitude to the many men and women who make their experience possible. This makes them more mindful of others who are serving them in other venues as well.

PRINCIPLE FOR MANHOOD: Thank every coach after every practice. Thank every coach and umpire (if possible, they often leave before the team has cleared the dugout) after every game. Thank the concession stand workers for their time. Thank the grounds crew (as available) for their work on the field. You will find yourself more grateful as you join your sons in their expressions of gratitude.

10. **Shake it off! Leadership and encouragement** A common expression from one player to another is to "shake it off" after a botched play or minor injury. Baseball requires a lot of mental toughness and good leadership on the field means you are encouraging teammates to "shake it off" to be ready for the next play. Typically, focusing on a failure in baseball means that you will not be focused on the next play, which means another failure.

PRINCIPLE FOR MANHOOD: Never correct another player while on the field. Good leaders on the field offer encouragement, and remember to keep a "short memory" and to "shake it off." Strategies for improvement can be discussed in the dugout.

11. **Father, where art thou? The decline of baseball** It is sad to me that one of the greatest sports is experiencing something of a decline at the youth recreation level. Some have argued that the proliferation of highly competitive travel teams have caused this demise. I think the socio-cultural phenomenon of absent fathers, however, has created the giant gap between recreation and competitive players and thereby created the need for more competitive venues. Baseball requires at least two people. You cannot play catch with yourself. You can't pitch to yourself, and you can't hit grounders to yourself. Normally this is where dad comes in. But where is he? Is he working too much, abandoning his family altogether, or is he just emotionally absent?

Over the next decade, fewer and fewer boys will enjoy the incredible father-son moments of playing catch, hitting grounders, spending hours discussing the nuances and character-building aspects of the game.

PRINCIPLE FOR MANHOOD: Encourage the church to stand in the gap and embrace the fatherless young men around you. Mentor them, teach them the gospel, and maybe toss the ball a time or two with them.

Win their hearts for the gospel

The tragedy in many homes today is that children grow up to be successful, but not in the things that matter most. With copious investment from their parents, they learn to behave well, collect numerous trophies, land nice scholarships to great colleges, and secure rewarding jobs, but don't have a discernible heart for God. This can also be true even when parents are intentional about raising boys to be biblically masculine men and raising girls to be biblically feminine women but aren't intentional about cultivating their children's relationship with God to find out why he made them that way.

> "One overarching purpose should drive your leadership as a father: molding your children's hearts for the gospel."

One overarching purpose should drive your leadership as a father: molding your children's hearts for the gospel. This is the instruction of Ephesians 6:4: "Fathers, do not provoke your children to anger, but bring them up in the discipline and instruction of the Lord." This means being faithful in discipline as well as in relating with your children's hearts.

It's never enough to just focus on behavior — to train children to obey you immediately, to sit up straight, not interrupt, do their schoolwork faithfully, and so on. You have to do a work in their heart. As you've probably heard along the way, rules without relationship lead to rebellion. This is especially true as your children move past the stage where they are fairly easy to control physically. Once they start experiencing more freedoms, you have to increasingly lead them through the influence of an engaging relationship.

This is all tied to winning and shaping your children's hearts. "My son, give me your heart," Solomon writes in the Proverbs, "and let your eyes observe my ways" (Prov 23:26). This is something that happens

> "Yes, childeren need to clean their room, to share with their brother, and to stop hitting, but more importantly, they need the gospel."

as you intentionally engage with your children day in and day out — not just in quality time, but in quantity time. It's being close enough to patiently discern when it's most appropriate to admonish, encourage or help your children (1 Thess 5:14).

It's also tied to proactively instructing in the areas of heart and character — the forces that drive your children's behaviors and influence the decisions they make. Instead of being a control freak who tries to micromanage your children, it means coaching them to make good decisions when you're not around and then giving them opportunities to put that coaching into practice through new learning and training experiences.

In the same way that rules without relationship leads to rebellion, we also know that a relationship with Christ is not built on following rules but on following a person. We have to cultivate in our children an ability to trust and follow us so that we can help them trust and follow Christ.

In all this relationship building, there is still a place for rules in winning your children's hearts for God. As rules without relationship leads to rebellion, we also learn in the book of Hebrews, that relationship without rules leads to illegitimacy: "For what son is there whom his father does not discipline? If you are left without discipline, in which all have participated, then you are illegitimate children and not sons (Heb 12:7b-8).

Discipline begins at the earliest ages as you require your children to obey without delay (they can't wait to obey when it's convenient for them), without disgust (they should be respectful in their obedience), and without discussion (they don't get to lay out all the reasons they don't want to obey or postpone obedience until they have all their "why" questions answered).

This approach to discipline not only brings consistency and order to your home, but it prepares children for Christ in two ways. First, it is a high enough standard that it gives you the opportunity to present the gospel on a regular basis. Every time your child fails to obey immediately, respectfully, and without talking back you can remind them that God's standard is perfection but we blow it because our hearts are inclined to evil. Every encounter of discipline is an opportunity to not only focus on the disobedience at hand, but on your children's need for a savior to redeem their rebellious hearts. Yes, they need to clean their room, to share with their brother and to stop hitting, but more importantly, they need the gospel.

Finally, teaching children to obey immediately, respectfully, and without debate prepares them to obey God in that same way. Too many young adults are struggling to obey God because their parents never disciplined them to obey immediately. So they end up like Jonah, running away from what God prompts them to do, or never taught them to obey with respect (so they are begrudging and complaining when they do obey), or they never had to obey without question (and so they feel entitled to know from God exactly why they should obey and what's in it for them before they'll decide whether or not to obey).

Cultivating in your children both a discipline of faithful obedience and a heart-level relationship in which they trust and follow you prepares them to trust and follow God and to welcome his discipline. Raising children like that — who are waking as faithful children of God — is the only kind of success that really matters. ∞

A

—

GUIDE

—

FOR

—

PASTORS

Shepherd your men

So I exhort the elders among you, as a fellow elder and a witness of the sufferings of Christ, as well as a partaker in the glory that is going to be revealed: shepherd the flock of God that is among you, exercising oversight, not under compulsion, but willingly, as God would have you; not for shameful gain, but eagerly; not domineering over those in your charge, but being examples to the flock. (1 Pet 5:1-2)

There's a lot to like about the current renaissance of manhood and it's no surprise that it's been making it's way into the Christian culture. Some see tapping into this movement as a way to get men to re-engage with the local church following years of declining male attendance.

But if you're a pastor or a lay leader of men in the local church, it's important to be wise about how you tap into this resurgence in manhood. It's not about just enjoying manly stuff. It's not about trying to beef up your manly persona or add street cred to your men's ministry. The last thing you want to do is motivate someone to be a man without calling them to be a man of God.

Remember the warning Peter gives: "Be sober-minded; be watchful. Your adversary the devil prowls around like a roaring lion, seeking someone to devour" (1 Pet 5:8). This is a warning to you personally, but Peter wrote it originally for shepherds of God's flock. There's a lion prowling around your church and community. His targets are passive men, preoccupied husbands, and disengaged dads. If marriage is to reflect Christ and the Church, Satan will go after husbands and try to make them lie about how Christ loves. If God reveals himself as "Father," Satan will tempt dads to portray God as distracted, harsh, and inconsistent. The gospel is at stake.

As men go, so goes the church. So, shepherd men. Don't just tap into the manhood resurgence with some manly activities here and there in your church. Build a church culture that will call boys and men to lives of self-sacrifice as exampled by the picture of Christ in Ephesians 5 who loved the church and gave himself for her to His own neglect and sacrifice. Have a burden to reach families through dads. Cultivate fathers who will disciple their children at home. Be a pastor who will boldly preach about and press for an ethos that expects this type of behavior from the men of your church. Require boys and men to do hard things, to cultivate toughness, resilience, and courage.

Strong men produce strong churches. So, shepherd men.

So what does that look like? How can you build a culture of biblical manhood in your church? It's both simpler and more challenging than you might think. Here are the essentials:

PREACH TO THE MEN IN YOUR CHURCH

Your ministry to men begins with proclamation of the Word from the pulpit. No program or special event can come close to the power of proclaiming God's Word. As you faithfully exegete Scripture to your congregation, be intentional about calling out men wherever applicable in a service.

For example, when you're talking about purity, don't leave your message generic. Say, "Listen to this, young men..." and point out God's distinct word for them. Look for opportunities to say, "This is for you husbands..." "God is speaking to fathers here..." Obviously, you can do the same thing for women and children, but don't miss the opportunity to drive home your application for men.

One way you can remember to do this is to put names and/or pictures of specific men from your church on your desk to have in view as you're preparing a message. Pray over those men and mediate on 1 Thessalonians 5:14: "Admonish the idle, encourage the fainthearted, help the weak, be patient with them all." Let the Spirit lead you to deliver the admonishment, encouragement, and help that your men need most.

CREATE AN APPETITE

"Men don't follow programs," writes blogger Tim Challies, "they follow men." Before you worry about structure and strategy, you have to grow a desire in your men.

Here are some ways you can do that:

- **Expose the enemy:** Men need to be reminded of what's at stake. Even though our surroundings are often comfortable and peaceful, we need to remember that the world is a battleground, not a playground. And we need to think like soldiers (2 Tim 2:1-4). One way to demonstrate to men what our spiritual enemy is like is to call some men together for a viewing of a movie like National Geographic's "Relentless Enemies." Read 1 Timothy 5:8, watch the movie, discuss, grow a movement.

- **Leave a vacuum:** One pastor we know made the need for servant-minded men dramatically obvious one Sunday morning. Men weren't stepping up to teach Sunday School and so he left the pulpit empty and went to teach the fifth grade class.

- **Plan a man camp:** Put together a man camp as a time to get your men together and in a setting where you can give them some targeted messages and grow their appetite. Keep it simple. Call some men out personally to be there and then make some intentional connections between men who could sharpen each other. In the process, draw out some older men and connect them with young men.

Whatever you do, don't over-promise and then under-deliver. Instead, start taking small, intentional steps that create an appetite and then feel free to over-deliver.

RESOURCE YOUR MEN

We are people of the Word. Foster a literate congregation — one with a love for the Word of God, as well as good books that illuminate the world God has given us:

- **Talk about books:** Quote good books in the pulpit. Ask men what they're reading. Blog about the books you recommend to men. Get men together and go through books together.

- **Give books away:** Buy up copies of great books and stick them in men's chests and challenge them to read it: "I don't know if you're man enough for this book." Create an appetite with shorter books like C.J. Mahaney's *Sex, Romance and the Glory of God* (or even this guidebook).

MODEL IT

Remember, more is caught than taught. Let your life serve as an open book — how you lead in the church, the community, your marriage and your family:

- **Get in the middle of the life of men in your church.** Don't try to shepherd by remote control. Have a meal or coffee with men from your church two to three times a week.

- **Don't complain in the pulpit.** Don't preface a sermon complaining about a cold or a late night. Grab the pulpit and preach through it.
- **Don't let the men around you complain.** Don't let men get away with making excuses when it's just a matter of life happening to them in a Genesis 3 world. If necessary, take them to the cancer ward to give them some healthy perspective.
- **Don't grumble about work to do — get at it.** Go for the heaviest stuff at the church work day. Don't let problems fester in your church, go after them.

SERVE ALL OF YOUR MEN

Esteem the men of your church better than yourselves. All of your men. Not just the people you like. That's a position of spiritual leadership in the context of the local church. It includes both the fun saints and the funky saints (and every church has them). God blesses us with them and you serve them too — not just your demographic.

"The parts of the body that seem to be weaker are indispensable," Paul told the Corinthians, adding, "God has so composed the body,

> "Esteem the men of your church better than yourselves. All of your men. Not just the people you like."

giving greater honor to the part that lacked it, that there may be no division in the body, but that the members may have the same care for one another. If one member suffers, all suffer together; if one member is honored, all rejoice together" (I Cor 12:22, 24-26).

So serve them all — until every man is mature in Christ (Col 1:28). This is what heaven is going to look like. Like the disciples who followed Christ, it's messy, but your goal as a shepherd is to cultivate unity, not uniformity.

CREATE CHALLENGES AND OPPORTUNITIES

You cannot just put a bunch of men together and assign them to a care group like some sort of E-Harmony for men and think that is going to help the masculine soul. We have modeled most of our men's ministries after our women's ministries — get the men together, read a book together, hold hands, and pray together and talk about the worst sin that you ever did — and that ain't happening. Men solve problems. They fix stuff. They get stuff done.

Don't put ant hills in front of the men of your church. Don't limit your men with weak assignments — on the bereavement, flower, grounds, or fellowship committees — give men a God-sized task that they know requires a man.

Come up with two or three projects, such as taking care of widows and orphans in your church, risky missions, or building projects. Call some men out individually to lead in these efforts — if you give a general invitation you'll typically get a general (and negligible) response.

Don't worry about having all the details in place before you get started. Just pull a few men together and give them a problem to solve. For instance, as winter approaches, you can say, "Let's check on all the widows in our church and see if they all have adequate warmth for the winter." One might need a new furnace. That might leave you wondering where a new furnace would come from. Figure it out. Solve the problem. That's what men do.

You could even plan some regular efforts like shoveling snow for elderly women as a group of men and then go have lunch at Five Guys (or another favorite restaurant). Enjoy a job well done and the camaraderie of taking on shared projects and challenges for the kingdom.

FILL IN STRATEGY AND STRUCTURE

Once you've been preaching and teaching it, modeling it, creating the desire and organizing man-sized projects for a while, you should have enough organic growth driving things to require you to come back and flesh out strategy and structure. If you focus on strategy and structure too much on the front end, you'll grow too programmatic and your structure will get in the way of ministry.

When you have a thriving, growing movement, that's the time to come back with some organization to make it sustainable. Strategy and structure at this point will help you guide and institutionalize what's happening. One thing to consider as you're institutionalizing things is what messages your church is sending to men visually — in your bulletin, your foyer and even your illustration designs on screen. Like Christian bookstores, these areas tend to target women, but can usually be made more focused

Autopsy of men in the church
• Tired and stressed
• Chasing idols of success
• Spiritually weak
• Committed to values but not Christ
• Unaccountable
• No integrity
• Preoccupied

on men without making women less engaged in your service.

Institutionalize it. But only after it's taken shape.

HELP MEN TAKE IT HOME

Finally, be intentional about helping your men lead as husbands and fathers.

Take men out for coffee or lunch and ask, "How does your leadership look at home?" Expect them to be facing challenges of some kind, but help them make movement. It doesn't have to be a touchdown, just start with some one-yard plays.

One way to find out how things are going in a man's marriage is to say, "Tell me about your last date with your wife." This is usually a pretty good barometer for where the marriage is. It also gives you an opportunity to offer date suggestions. A good way to serve the men in your church is to keep handy a list of ideas for local dates. Remind the men who get this list, however, that it's to be kept secret — as a code of honor among the men of your church. Your wives don't need to know about this shared intelligence.

As you look to invest in men as fathers, we encourage you to explore the great work God is doing through models that intentionally connect church and home. At Southern Seminary, for instance, we've outlined a vision for families called the "Family Equipping Ministry Model." Family-equipping ministry is a process of realigning a congregation's proclamation and practices so that parents — especially fathers — are acknowledged, trained, and held accountable as persons primarily responsible for their children's discipleship. It reorients every ministry to partner with parents in the task of discipleship. (see more at http://www.sbts.edu/family/)

We hope you'll find this model to be helpful, but most importantly, we hope you'll be committed to shepherding the men of your church on a regular basis — admonishing and encouraging them toward biblical manhood and disciple making for the glory of God. ◇◇◇

Final encouragement: Don't give up

It's not easy to stay engaged in biblical manhood — to bring faithful leadership to yourself, your family, your community, or your church. Often, the more you seek to lead, the harder it gets. But you will reap a harvest if you don't give up.

"Do not be deceived," Paul writes to the Galatians, "God is not mocked, for whatever one sows, that will he also reap. For the one who sows to his own flesh will from the flesh reap corruption, but the one who sows to the Spirit will from the Spirit reap eternal life. And let us not grow weary of doing good, for in due season we will reap, if we do not give up" (Gal 6:7-9).

There are three vital truths from this passage as you seek to faithfully live out your manhood for the glory of God:

YOU REAP WHAT YOU SOW: We mock God when we do the wrong thing (or just sit on the sidelines) and expect no consequences. We also mock God when we think there will be no fruit. But God is not mocked: you will harvest a crop in the future one way or the other. You can reap a fruitful and bountiful harvest or a weed and thorn-infested wasteland, but you *will* reap what you sow.

YOU REAP MORE THAN YOU SOW: In God's generosity, he allows us to reap more than we sow. Many of us will enjoy reaping the benefits of the sowing done by our parents or the parents of the women we marry. We'll enjoy harvests in our churches from the faithful sowing of generations before. Even more so, when we sow to the Spirit, we will reap eternal life — a harvest beyond anything we could ever sow in our own strength and understanding.

YOU REAP LATER THAN YOU SOW: You sow in one season and reap in another. We've heard men say, "I've been trying to lead in my family for three months now and it's just not working." But it's not a matter of months, it's years. There's no immediate gratification in sowing and reaping. There is fruit in it if you'll stay at it, but it takes patient cultivation.

"See how the farmer waits for the precious fruit of the earth, being patient about it, until it receives the early and the late rains," writes James, "You also, be patient" (Jas 5:7b-8a).

And even as you wait, you have to work by the sweat of your brow and sow in ground that's filled with thorns and thistles. It's not easy. Expect it to be messy and filled with challenges and setbacks along the way. Sowing in biblical manhood is disruptive stuff. But don't give up. Be obedient and faithful: "And let us not grow weary of doing good, for in due season we will reap, if we do not give up."

Even as you work in hope of a future harvest, you can have the joy of going to sleep every night exhausted from leading but knowing that instead of wasting your manhood, you are living out your original purpose and assignment as God's man in your home, your work and your local church. ∞∞∞

RESOURCES

FURTHER READING

Manly Dominion by Mark Chanski
Masculine Mandate: God's Call to Men by Richard Phillips
What's the Difference? Manhood and Womanhood Defined According to the Bible by John Piper
Pastoral Leadership for Biblical Manhood and Womanhood edited by Wayne Grudem and Dennis Rainey
Men and Women: Equal Yet Different by Alexander Strauch
Boyhood and Beyond: Practical Wisdom for Becoming a Man by Bob Schultz
Created for Work: Practical Insights for Young Men by Bob Schultz
Anchor Man, Point Man and **King Me** by Steve Farrar

After Patriarchy What?: Why Egalitarians Are Winning the Evangelical Gender Debate
by Russell D. Moore (www.russellmoore.com/documents/2005ETS.pdf)

Council on Biblical Manhood and Womanhood: www.CBMW.org

The Danvers Statement on Biblical Manhood and Womanhood: www.cbmw.org/Danvers

PUBLICATIONS OF SOUTHERN BAPTIST THEOLOGICAL SEMINARY

Towers: towers.sbts.edu
Southern Seminary Magazine: www.sbts.edu/friends-and-donors/magazine/
Journal of Family Ministry: www.sbts.edu/family/journal

THE SOUTHERN BAPTIST THEOLOGICAL SEMINARY
SBTS.edu
Facebook.com/TheSBTS
Twitter.com/SBTS
Instagram.com/SouthernSeminary

BOYCE COLLEGE
BoyceCollege.com
Facebook.com/BoyceCollege
Twitter.com/BoyceCollege
Instagram.com/BoyceCollege

THE SOUTHERN SEMINARY STORY:

At Southern Seminary, TRUTH is our foundation for learning and our LEGACY runs deep. Each year, thousands of students see their VISION come alive while fulfilling their ministry calling with us. We believe that we are living in serious times and we are looking for students who are serious about impacting our world with the gospel of Christ.

This guidebook is based on the class Biblical Masculinity offered by the seminary and taught by Randy Stinson and Dan Dumas.

GUIDEBOOK PRODUCTION:

Authors:

Randy Stinson — Randy Stinson is the senior vice president for Academic Administration and provost at The Southern Baptist Theological Seminary in Louisville, Kentucky. He also serves as the senior fellow of the Council on Biblical Manhood and Womanhood.

A recognized authority on the subject of biblical manhood and womanhood, Stinson is a regular conference speaker on the subjects of adoption, parenting, marriage, and men's leadership. He is the co-author of *A Guide to Biblical Manhood* and co-editor of *Trained in the Fear of God: Family Ministry in Theological, Historical, and Practical Perspective*.

In his spare time, he enjoys hunting, fishing, and encourages his children in their pursuits of baseball, tennis, and lacrosse.

He and his wife, Danna, have been married for 24 years and have eight children: Gunnar and Georgia (twin 18 year olds), Fisher (16), Eden (15), Payton (13), Spencer (10), Willa (9), and Brewer (9).

Dan Dumas — Dan Dumas is a teaching pastor and elder at Crossing Church in Louisville, Kentucky. He is passionate about leadership, expository preaching, biblical manhood, and being an idea-generating, transformational ministry architect. He is the co-author of *A Guide to Biblical Manhood* and the editor of *A Guide to Expository Ministry*. Dumas became a senior vice president and faculty member at Southern Seminary in 2007. Dan actively writes on Leadership and Preaching at his blog: Leaders Don't Panic, and provides a variety of coaching and consulting for businesses, churches, and their leaders. Dan has served in a variety of ministry capacities in many local churches, including executive pastor at Grace Community Church in Sun Valley, California. Prior to his time in ministry, Dan served in the US Navy as a search and rescue specialist.

Dan is married to Jane and has two children: Aidan (12) and Elijah (6). He loves all things sports (especially water sports) and is an avid outdoorsman who loves hunting and fly fishing.

Editor: **Steve Watters** — Steve Watters has been married to Candice for 18 years and is the father of four children. He and Candice created *Boundless Webzine* for Focus on the Family in 1998. They also co-wrote the book *Start Your Family: Inspiration for Having Babies*. Steve enjoys hiking, reading, and writing. Steve is vice-president for Communications at Southern Seminary.

Designer: **Tyler Deeb** — Tyler Deeb is the founder and designer of Misc Goods Co, which began in 2012. He has a background as an art director, designer, and illustrator. In 2004, he began actively pursuing graphic design work and founded his first design company, Pedale Design, in 2008. He has worked with a range of clients from start-ups to big businesses, advertising agencies, and nonprofit charities.

Printed in the United States of America

ISBN 978-0615469423

Made in the USA
San Bernardino, CA
14 June 2016